by HENRY GASSER, N. A.

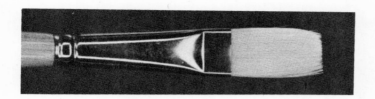

oil painting

methods and demonstrations

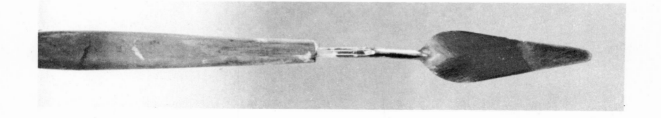

REINHOLD PUBLISHING CORPORATION • NEW YORK

TO

DR. JOHN S. HERRON

*in deep appreciation for his
encouragement and guidance*

TABLE OF CONTENTS

HENRY GASSER, *whose paintings are in more than twenty-six museum collections, including the Philadelphia, Boston, and Newark Museums, studied at the Newark School of Fine and Industrial Art, at the Grand Central School of Art, and at the Art Students League of New York. For more than twelve years his work has been exhibited throughout the United States and abroad, winning a number of important awards. Henry Gasser has also lectured and demonstrated painting techniques for art groups and schools in various parts of the country; at present he is the Director of the Newark School of Fine and Industrial Art. He is the author of the books* Casein Painting: Methods and Demonstrations *and* Watercolor—How to Do It.

Among the awards that Henry Gasser has received are the Hallgarten prize at the National Academy; the Zabriskie, Osborne, and Obrig prizes at the American Water Color Society; the Connecticut Academy first and second prizes; the silver and gold medals at Oakland, California; and various awards from the Audubon Artists, Salmagundi Club, and Philadelphia and Washington Water Color Clubs. He is a life member of the National Arts Club and the Art Students League as well as a member of a number of other art organizations, including the National Academy of Design, American Water Color Society, Salmagundi Club, Philadelphia Water Color Club, California Water Color Society, Baltimore Water Color Club, and Connecticut Academy. (Photo by Augusta Berns Bamberger Studio.)

INTRODUCTION

Years of teaching, directing an art school, and appearing before art groups throughout the country have led me to two firm conclusions.

The first is that serious students of landscape art are very much interested in the structure of a painting—how the artist arrives at a certain composition, how he achieves certain color effects, the painting sequence in building textures, what medium is used. They know that what goes on "behind the scenes," so to speak, is vital to the success of the work.

Secondly, I am convinced that actual demonstrations, accompanied by explanatory remarks, provide the quickest way for students to master the technical approach to painting. Here, as in so many fields, the visual "chalk-talk" method of instruction produces better results than does unrelieved lecturing.

Therefore, in this book, I have attempted to supply the student-artist with what—based on my experience through the years—I believe he wants to know: exactly how a painting is developed, step by step, from idea to finished art.

The step-by-step demonstrations that follow are of typical landscapes encountered everywhere. The subjects illustrated are literal renderings, enabling the student to understand more readily the elements that make up the picture.

The student will find separate chapters on composition, design, and the like, and he also will be guided in solving those problems while he follows each step-by-step demonstration.

Wherever possible, I have explained through illustration. Text has been kept to a minimum. I trust that this kind of presentation will be of maximum benefit to you, the student-artist!

PAINTING EQUIPMENT

In describing the following equipment I have listed only the basic requirements for oil painting.

In the art field there are several grades of material and equipment. Even the novice can judge the comparative value of such indispensable items as easels and paint boxes by looking at the workmanship and materials employed. More difficult is the selection of brushes and paints. In these items "name" brands must be considered if you want to be sure of getting quality material. Most of the manufacturers of these items have placed "student" and "artist" grade products on the market.

As colors and brushes form the most important part of your equipment, I have devoted separate chapters to their selection.

The following is a list of items that are needed preparatory to painting:

A paint or sketch box—12 inches by 16 inches
A palette (wood or metal) to fit the above box
A palette knife
A double oil cup
Canvas panels (to fit the paint box)
Canvas (see Various Painting Surfaces)
Stretcher strips
Charcoal sticks or charcoal pencils
A painting knife (see Palette Knife Painting)
Turpentine, oil, and varnish (see Painting Mediums)
Fixatif and an atomizer
Brushes (see Selection and Care of Brushes)
Paints (see Selection of Colors)

When purchasing a paint box, do not select one that has already been stocked with paints. It probably will include some colors you do not want. Paint boxes are obtainable that have only a palette which fits snugly into the box.

There is a disposable paper palette on the market that is becoming increasingly popular, especially among novices. It is made up of several sheets of paper, cut to the size and shape of the traditional palette, and bound in pad form. After using the top sheet, you simply tear it off and the next sheet is exposed, ready for use. However, most artists take a personal pride in the glossy working surface that a wood palette eventually acquires.

The palette knife is an indispensable tool. It is used to mix as well as to remove paint from the palette. Unwanted passages of color, whether wet or dry, can be removed from the canvas with the palette knife.

The use of the painting knife is given in full detail in a later chapter that fully demonstrates the various ways it can be handled.

The double oil cup is clipped to the palette; one cup is for the painting medium, the other for turpentine.

You can buy stretcher strips, generally made of white pine or cedar, in any desired combination of sizes. The most popular measurements range from 9 inches by 12 inches to 25 inches by 30 inches.

Make your drawing or preliminary compositional outlines with the stick of charcoal or charcoal pencil. A lead pencil can also be used, provided it is made of pure graphite. Any pencil that contains a substance such as indelible lead will come through the oil paint. When charcoal is used, it should be sprayed with a fixatif or else it should be dusted off lightly with a rag. Retain a faint image as a guide when you start the painting proper. Additional equipment that you can eventually acquire and which you will find useful is a pair of pliers expressly made for stretching canvas.

An item you will find very handy is a brush cleaner made of metal. It is designed with a strainer that separates the clear kerosene or turpentine from the sediment.

STUDIO EQUIPMENT

A substantial vertical easel is of major importance to you for studio use; it is better than a tripod sketching easel. The canvas rests solidly on the supporting shelf of the easel. This shelf can be raised or lowered to a comfortable working height, no matter what the size of the canvas you are painting. The canvas can also be tilted at any angle to eliminate the glare of wet paint.

Although most artists prefer to work from a standing position, you may wish to have a high stool available to rest on after several hours of painting. However, to paint regularly from a seated position tends to cramp a more vigorous approach when you are doing a large canvas. You should view a painting every so often from a distance—the larger the painting, the further the distance.

I might also mention at this time, as an aid in checking the progress of the painting, you should place it in a frame and view it at frequent intervals. Some artists do their entire studio painting with the canvas set in a frame. The placing of a painting in a frame in the latter stages acts as a guide in determining just how much finished detail is actually needed. Stock-size frames can be put aside for just this purpose.

A small table should be near the easel so that you can place the palette on it. Unless you are doing a portrait where a close contact of the mixing and matching of color from the sitter to the canvas is desirable, it is more convenient to work with the palette resting on the table. An artist's tabouret is more functional than a table because not only is it the correct working height, but it will hold all the necessary equipment in a minimum amount of space. With the palette placed on the flat-top surface of the tabouret, there is plenty of accessible drawer space for reserve brushes that may be needed during the course of the painting. Extra tubes of paint may also be stored in one of the drawers, and most tabourets have a small closet for keeping the various bottles of turpentine, linseed oil, varnishes, etc.

A studio with a steady north light is, of course, ideal. However, the source of light is not as important to the landscape painter when working in his studio as it is to the portrait painter. As long as there is sufficient light and the windows do not face the direct sunlight, which distorts the color, satisfactory painting can be accomplished.

Indeed, I often do a great deal of planning and preliminary work at night—considerable drawing and toning in of color values, compositional sketches, and the like.

After experimenting with various lighting arrangements, I have found that a combination of fluorescent and flood lights can approximate daylight working conditions. Care must be exercised when using yellow and certain blue paints, but it is surprising how far a subject can be carried under artificial light. The subtle color passages and the final painting are best done in daylight.

OUTDOOR EQUIPMENT

The weight of equipment you select for outdoor painting is important. In the course of searching for subjects to paint, do not be surprised to find that you may have to do quite a bit of walking before you come upon suitable material. There is no point in becoming exhausted carrying around a lot of heavy equipment. You will have little energy left for painting!

With your paint box already selected, you will need a folding or collapsible sketching easel. There are several models available, the most popular being those which are lightest in weight and which fold into a small compact unit. Whatever type you select, make certain that it has an overhead extension grip with which to fasten the easel to the top of the canvas. The easel should also be movable so that the canvas can be tilted at an angle to avoid the glare of the sun.

Strong, well-balanced, wooden easels with rust-proof hardware are the best, along with the newer all-aluminum models. Keep in mind that you will be painting many times in a strong wind and that a sturdy easel will be of great aid under such conditions. You will need a sketching stool if you prefer to work in a sitting position. These are also available both in metal and in wood. A metal chair with a cloth seat makes a compact and comfortable stool.

If you sit while working, you can place your palette on top of the sketch box in front of you. Or, again, you can work with the sketch box in your lap, using the lid as an easel. If you stand, it will be necessary to hold the palette, unless you have an especially designed easel. As the subject often decides for you whether it can be viewed better from a sitting or from a standing position, I think that it is wise to have a sketching stool available—the chance of finding a convenient substitute like a rock is rather remote!

Always check your equipment before starting out on a sketching trip. To be found short on white, yellow ochre, or blue is extremely awkward when attempting to do a painting from nature. Carry as many canvas panels as you can fit into your sketching box. While you may intend to use only one, it is just possible that you may get off to a bad start! It is often easier to switch to a clean canvas and start anew than to attempt to keep working on the initial effort. Again, as I mention in a later chapter, an extra panel will enable you to conclude the day's work with a quick sketch or supplementary study.

Carry several paint rags and save one for the end of the day's work. You can wrap it around brushes and so prevent the sketching box from becoming smeared with paint. As an additional precaution, dip the rag in clean turpentine to keep the brushes flexible until you can wash them with soap and water.

A small pad for pencil notes should complete your sketching equipment. It takes up little room and is invaluable in planning preliminary compositions and for making important notations.

THE SELECTION OF COLORS

While you have undoubtedly already acquired the materials for painting, a review of essential colors may be in order.

The following permanent colors, selected for a basic landscape palette, are suggested:

Alizarin crimson	Light red
Cadmium yellow light	French ultramarine
Cadmium red light	Ivory black
Yellow ochre	Viridian
Zinc or titanium white	

These colors can be supplemented by:

Cadmium yellow deep	Raw sienna
Cadmium orange	Burnt umber
Cobalt blue	Burnt sienna
Cerulean blue	Oxide of chromium, opaque

Many of the leading manufacturers of paints carry both an artist's and a student's line of colors. The student grade is less expensive and will answer most purposes. However, whenever possible, use the artist's grade, as it possesses far greater covering power and color intensity.

As you progress, you will in all probability want to discard some of the colors listed above or add new ones to your palette. By all means do so, as long as those selected are listed as permanent. The phthalocyanine colors of green and blue can be used to good effect in landscape painting, but you must employ them with discretion, for their strong staining power often overwhelms the other colors. Indian red, cerulean blue, or possibly the mars colors may be found suitable for certain purposes. As black is a notoriously slow-drying color, however sparingly used, I have recently switched to the mars black because it dries more rapidly. There are other factors that will influence you to extend your range of colors. When painting outdoors, you wish to capture on canvas as soon as possible the everchanging effect of nature. With a wider range of colors to choose from, you may be able to work faster because you need less time in mixing a particular shade.

You will want to use fast-drying colors when you prepare an underpainting in the studio. Oxide of chromium and the umbers will then be of great aid. The chapter on underpainting lists additional colors that are helpful when using this approach. As you gain experience, you will automatically discard colors when you discover that you can achieve similar effects with new combinations of your basic palette of colors. While you should always be interested, of course, in the possibilities of any new colors that may be developed, eventually you will settle down to a favorite personal palette. Then all you will be concerned with is concentrating on the important aspects of picture making!

The arrangement of colors

The colors can be laid out on the palette in any number of ways convenient for painting. However, once an arrangement is arrived at, you should keep the colors in that order. Having a definite place for each color on the palette establishes the habit of being able to locate the desired color automatically, with a minimum amount of fumbling.

The two diagrams below show arrangements for the basic as well as for the advanced palette. In both, the warm colors are laid out along the top edge of the palette and the cool colors along the left side. As the top edge is the long side of the palette and warm colors are generally more numerous, the additional space is an advantage. A double cup is clipped on the right side. One cup holds the copal painting medium, and turpentine can be

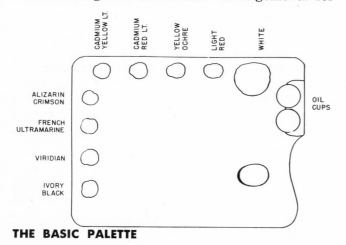

THE BASIC PALETTE

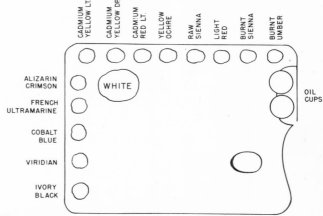

THE ADVANCED PALETTE

placed in the other. The latter is of particular aid when sketching outdoors and it is necessary to clean a brush quickly.

When I am working on a large canvas and using a full range of colors, I place the white paint below and to the right of the arrangement. Besides enabling me to lay out a larger amount of white paint, this location makes mixing easier, and after a day's work the white can be removed easily.

The rest of the colors can remain, as most paints are usable for some time. However, the white invariably becomes stained and it is better to remove it, along with the used mixtures that cover the working space.

It is very important that this working space be thoroughly cleaned at the end of the working day. Use a rag to wipe the palette after the surplus paint has been removed with the palette knife.

The palette knife is used to keep the working area of the palette clean.

PAINTING MEDIUMS

A painting medium is used with oil paint to help manipulate the pigment, to attain certain effects, and to change the paint's consistency. Some mediums are used to accelerate the drying time of paint, others to retard it.

For straight painting I prefer a copal oil painting mixture made up of one-third copal oil varnish, one-third linseed oil, and one-third turpentine.

There is a prepared copal painting medium available that is excellent for all-around use, from the thinning of the pigments at the start of the painting to the final glazing.

Various ingredients used in oil painting mediums are:

STAND OIL, being of heavy consistency, must be thinned with turpentine to attain a free brushing quality. It imparts an enamel-like finish to the painting and is non-yellowing.

SUN-THICKENED OR SUN-REFINED OIL dries faster than stand oil. It can be thinned with turpentine, and it dries with a gloss.

COBALT DRIER can be added in a very small amount to the painting medium to accelerate the drying of paints. It is very helpful when mixed with the slow-drying stand oil. It should be mixed

thoroughly with the paint and used only when the latter is applied to the canvas in thin layers. Too much drier will affect the permanence of the painting.

OIL OF CLOVES can be used to retard the drying of paints. It should be used most sparingly, as too much oil of cloves will cause the picture to darken.

TURPENTINE is used to cut the consistency of the paint as well as to speed its drying. Only the pure gum spirits or rectified turpentine should be used. Excessive use of just turpentine alone will weaken the adherence of the paint film.

It can be deduced from the above notes that it is safer to use painting mediums as sparingly as possible. To omit medium entirely, however, makes the workability of the paint as it comes from the tube very difficult.

Subjects such as still-lifes and posed figures that I painted more than 15 years ago were accomplished without the use of medium. They are as fresh today as when they were painted.

However, in the doing of landscapes, especially those painted on the spot, where effects are fleeting and weather conditions often hinder the working of the paint, medium is of great help.

THE SELECTION AND CARE OF BRUSHES

Most landscape painting is done with bristle brushes. They come in various sizes, ranging in widths from $\frac{1}{8}$ inch to 2 inches. They are divided into three types: long hair brushes known as "flats," short brushes "brights," and round brushes. While bristle brushes bear the brunt of the work, being much tougher than the softer sable brushes, the latter are also important in achieving certain effects. They are most useful for the blending of paint and are less likely to disturb the surface of any wet underpainting. On the other hand, a novice's inexperienced use of sable brushes is apt to impart a superficial slickness to his work.

It is better to do as much work as possible with bristle brushes. They should be of sufficient size so that a broad, rather than a niggly, approach is acquired.

The choice of the size of brushes is a personal one, depending upon the canvas size and your working method.

The following is a substantial selection of brushes:
Bristle Brushes
  Numbers—2, 4, 7 (round)
  Numbers—2, 4, 6, 8, 10 (flats and brights)
Flat Sable Brushes
  As the identifying numbers often vary according to the manufacturer, the width is given—$\frac{1}{4}$ inch, $\frac{1}{2}$ inch, $\frac{3}{4}$ inch.

Over a period of time you will gradually add more brushes to your collection. Every size and type can be used. Place them in a large jar with their working end up and within easy reach from your easel. It is essential to keep them clean. Take particular heed that no paint becomes imbedded where the hairs meet the ferrule.

At the end of the day's work your brushes should be thoroughly washed in lukewarm water with a mild soap. Rub the hairs of the brushes on the soap and then work up a lather on the palm of your hand. Take one brush at a time and rub the soapy lather well into the hair. Make certain that all of the paint is dislodged, especially at the ferrule. Then rinse thoroughly with clear cool running water. Squeeze the surplus moisture from the brush with the thumb and forefinger and at the same time reshape it to its original contours. If you take good care of your brushes, they should last a long time. Even when they become thin and worn, they are useful for achieving certain effects and textures.

If the paint should dry hard in a brush, use a good paint remover to soften it. Make certain that a good washing of lukewarm water and soap follows, with the usual pressing of the brush into its original shape.

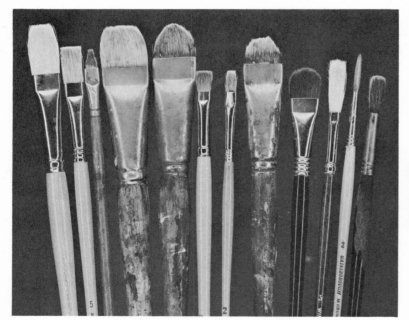 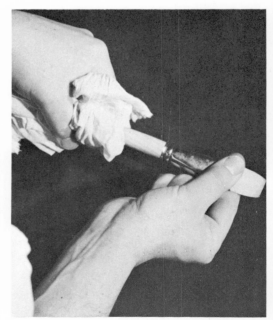

The photograph on the left above shows a group of typical brushes used for oil painting. Even as your favorite brush wears down, it can serve a purpose by achieving certain effects impossible to obtain with a new brush.

The photo on the right illustrates the squeezing of the hairs of the brush to remove all surplus moisture after the brush has been thoroughly washed. It is then placed upright in a container and allowed to dry.

THE USE OF THE VARIOUS BRUSHES

Long-Haired Bristle

This brush is known as a "flat" and shares the brunt of the painting chores with the shorter-haired bristle shown below. More flexible than the latter, the flat possesses a springy quality that can produce a very fluid brush stroke.

Short-Haired Bristle

Known as "brights," the short, stiff hairs of this bristle brush have a tendency to dig into a previously painted wet surface. However, for direct painting outdoors when speed is necessary to capture fleeting effects, you will find that this brush is indispensable. A thin line can be obtained by using the edge of the brush, and its stiff qualities may be made use of in quickly scooping the paint from palette and applying it vigorously to the canvas.

Outline Brush

A flat bristle brush is useful for outlining or drawing the composition on your canvas. When sketching outdoors, artists prefer the small size pictured here. A variety of lines can be obtained, from a heavy one by using the flat side of the brush to a thin line by using the brush edgewise.

11

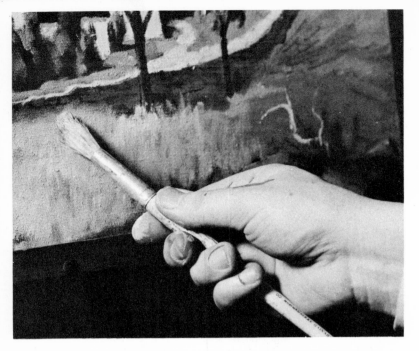

Round Bristle

Although the round bristle brush does not enjoy the popularity it once did, it can serve many purposes. It will not hold as much paint as the flat and bright bristle brushes, but you will find it useful for obtaining textural effects where a rough or stippled surface is desired.

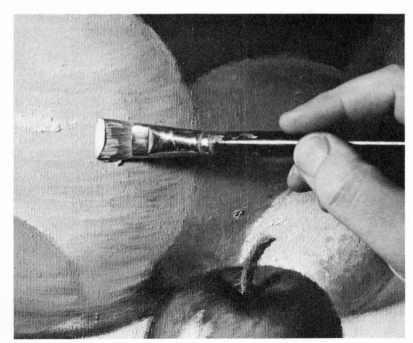

Round Sable

This brush is most useful in depicting a variety of fine lines. Held loosely near the end of the handle, it allows a free flowing line to be obtained. Gripping it pencil-like by the ferrule, you can apply a controlled, minute accent. A small rigger brush, possessing a chiseled edge in contrast to the pointed round sable brush, may also be found useful.

Flat Sable

This brush is excellent for glazing and where you want a high degree of finish. It is particularly effective when you are working on a smooth surface such as a gesso panel. It is useful when you wish to superimpose one color over another without disturbing the passage painted just before.

Filbert

The filbert combines several of the characteristics of the flat and round bristle brush. The resiliency of the soft sable filbert is of extreme help when doing a casein underpainting for which water is used as the medium. There is also less tendency to pile up paint when using this brush, making it desirable for any underpainting that must necessarily be kept thin. The filbert will be found to be a useful brush for all mediums.

House Painter's Brush

For the covering of large areas, backgrounds and rough toning work at the preliminary stages of a large canvas, the house painter's brush is a time saver. The one inch will be found best for these purposes. A softer hair brush of the same width will be found ideal for applying retouch and final coats of varnish.

Badger Blender

Indicative of its name, this brush is useful for smooth blending of colors after they have been applied to the canvas with the regular painting brushes. You will also find it handy for blurred or different effects such as the edges of distant foliage, etc.

13

Palette Knife

Besides being used for removing paint to be discarded from the palette, you can use the palette knife for a similar purpose directly on the canvas. When you find that you have accumulated too much paint in an area and that the color is still incorrect, it is better to scrape it off and start anew.

Pointed Knife

Handled carefully, as well as sparingly, the knife can be used where finely textured lines are required on a wet or dry surface. Use the sharp edge of the knife to remove dried paint in small areas.

Back of the Brush

Even the wooden part of the brush can be employed as a textural device. So long as the painted surface is still wet, the pointed end can be used like the knife. It produces a coarser line, useful in depicting light-stemmed foliage, grass, etc. It is most effective on a heavily painted surface.

THE VARIOUS PAINTING SURFACES

Stretched canvas

Durability, sympathetic texture, and convenience make a stretched canvas the most popular working surface.

Canvas is made of linen or cotton. The latter is definitely less durable and has, as well, an inferior, unpleasant working surface. Linen, however, is more expensive, so cotton is often substituted — especially by students and novices. There are linen-cotton mixtures available, but in working with them I have found that they possess an uneven absorption. The surface of cotton canvas can be improved by giving it an additional coating of white lead paint. To do this, first stretch the canvas on strips of the size preferred. Then, using a first-class make of white lead paint, obtainable in pound cans, spread it over the entire cotton surface. The white lead should be cut with copal or retouch varnish and the spreading done with the palette knife. Keep the coating thin, using the edge of the knife in a fan-like motion to distribute the white lead paint evenly. Allow to dry — generally a week will suffice — and then the canvas is ready for use.

When you purchase canvas by the roll, keep in mind your probable working sizes. For example, a 42-inch roll will give you an economical cut. This is obtained by cutting the 42-inch measurement to 22 inches, leaving 20 inches. The first measurement will make up a 20 by 24 size canvas, and the latter an 18 by 24 size. The inch margin on each side is necessary for gripping the canvas when stretching it over the wooden strips.

When selecting the texture of the canvas, the rule is that, generally, the smaller the working size, the smoother the canvas. However, fairly rough surfaces lend themselves to more sympathetic treatment of landscape subjects. When you tack the canvas to the stretcher, try to have it smooth enough so that it is not necessary to use the keys for additional tautness. Rather, use the keys to tighten the canvas if any slacking takes place later.

Canvas-covered boards

Canvas-covered boards do not possess as attractive a working surface as the resilient stretched canvas, but they are very convenient for outdoor sketching. They take up very little room and the 12 inch by 16 inch size fits into the average paint box. Most canvas boards are made of cotton; the extra coating of white lead mentioned previously will reduce their absorbency.

Manufactured textured panels

There are always new panels available on the market that contain simulated canvas textures embossed upon their surfaces. These panels may be made of paper, composition board, or cardboard. Their lasting qualities are most doubtful, but being low in price and light in weight, they do have a popular budget appeal. Their machine-made surfaces are inclined to give a monotonous look to the painting, particularly if the paint has been applied thinly. However, they can be used for sketching purposes or when permanence is not a factor.

Presdwood (masonite)

Presdwood is a reliable product that can be purchased from any building supply firm. It has a rough and a smooth side, the latter preferred for painting purposes. It is manufactured in sheets 4 feet wide and comes in lengths up to 12 feet.

Several thicknesses are available, with the 1/8 inch measurement most suitable. The smooth side should first be rubbed with a course sandpaper to roughen its surface. Then give it a coating of white lead, thinned with a copal varnish and applied with a brush. You will need at least two coats to cover the brown undertone. Each additional coat can be applied when the previous one is dry (generally applied one day apart if the coats are sufficiently thinned down). Allow the same interval of a week, as when coating the cotton canvas, before using the board for painting.

Gesso panels

Details on gesso panels are given in the chapter demonstrating their use. They can be obtained ready-made but are generally too absorbent for direct oil painting. This absorbency can be reduced by giving the panel a coating of shellac. The shellac should first be thinned with alcohol to a watery consistency. As the gesso has a tendency to "pull" the brush, it is not the best surface to use for quickly capturing effects when painting outdoors.

It is excellent, however, for studio painting, its surface imparting a great luminosity to oil glazes.

COLOR

Light, the source of color

All of us have witnessed a scene that sparkled with life and vitality, but viewed again at a later date, it looked drab and colorless.

The first time we had come upon the scene when the light was most effective, bringing forth a full play of color and a pleasing arrangement of shadow, both combining to enhance the subject. Upon seeing it the second time, the light had changed completely and with it the previous effect. You can make interesting studies of how the light affects the same subject in a single day. Morning and late afternoon will generally be found best for average subjects, with the overhead light of noon being the least flattering. We learn a bit about how color is determined by the quantity of light as we conclude these studies with an evening scene. For observing the quality of light, these studies are made of the same subject on different days. We discover that on a sunny day the local color of an object is absorbed by the strong glare and the feeling of sunlight is conveyed mainly by the strongly cast shadows.

On a sunless day the diffused light eliminates the cast shadows, but the local color becomes more apparent.

On a foggy day the weak light causes objects to become less distinct, their corners lost and the color greyed.

So far our studies have included the way in which light affects the local color of a subject during one day as well as on several days. Now let us observe how the seasons change the color of our subject. The plate on the right page shows the painting of the same subject during the four seasons—spring, summer, autumn, and winter. Lighting conditions have been chosen that are typical for each season.

Our first impression of the scene during the early spring is one of sprouting fresh green grass breaking the brown earth, contrasting with the greyed washed out, but hardy grass that has survived the winter snow. With most of the trees still bare of leaves and others just starting to blossom, their anatomy is clearly revealed to you. Observe the rolling contours of the hills, which, in summer, seem to be just a mass of green, but are now revealed as individual shapes of varying size and color, all intertwining to form a series of harmonious patterns.

Next we come to the summer scene, with its verdant foliage where everything appears to be a mass of green to the eyes of the novice. A penetrating search for the subtle coloring of various greens should be made.

Warm and cool greens must be sought and their yellows and blues forced, if necessary, to define them. For example, when attempting to separate the various greens and one is a warm yellow, stress the yellow hue; if a cool bluish green, stress the blue hue.

When observing and painting the autumn version, almost the opposite holds true. Now we have such a variety of colors that restraint has to be used when transposing them to the canvas. It is now that we seek the various greys to act as a foils for the bright colors. It is impossible to reproduce on your canvas the full brilliancy of color that is before you. By judicial use of the greys and careful spotting of bright color, the latter is enhanced. A brilliant vibrancy results through contrast that would be impossible to achieve by merely placing bright raw colors on the canvas.

At first glance the blanket of snow that covers the winter subject seems to simplify the scene to the viewer. This very simplicity is most deceiving when the painting is to be done. Far more is needed than white paint and blue-violet shadows! The winter scene allows the painter to run the full range of color values from extreme light to the darkest dark. The difficulty is arriving at the values in between.

On certain winter days the trees, whose local color would be brown or deep grey, appear black in contrast to the white of the snow. Yet the modeling of the contours of the snow must be painted graduations of the tone and color between those contrasts. It is when you establish those graduations convincingly that you learn that snow is only relatively white!

As we sum up the result of our studies of a subject under varying lighting conditions, time of day, and season of year, we learn the following:

That color is never actually the same on consecutive days.

That color is strong in the foreground and it weakens as it recedes.

That color is more harmonious when a mantle of subdued light envelops the subject.

That color gives variety to a scene.

That the color of the sky is a vital factor in the color scheme.

That all color is relative to its surrounding color.

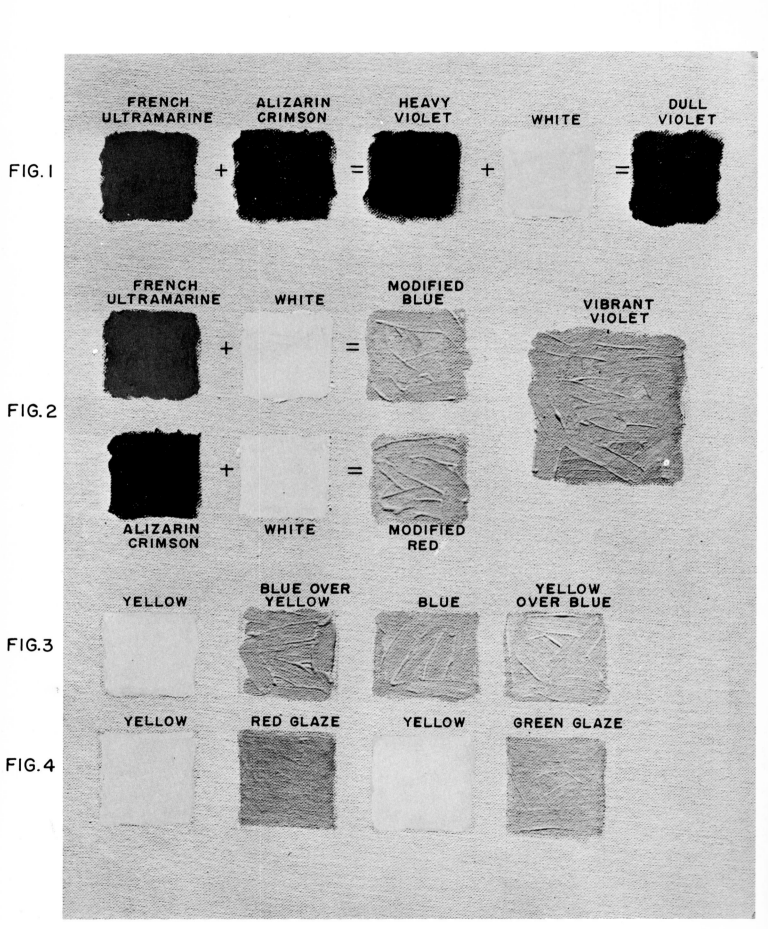

FIG.1   FRENCH ULTRAMARINE + ALIZARIN CRIMSON = HEAVY VIOLET + WHITE = DULL VIOLET

FIG.2   FRENCH ULTRAMARINE + WHITE = MODIFIED BLUE   VIBRANT VIOLET

ALIZARIN CRIMSON + WHITE = MODIFIED RED

FIG.3   YELLOW   BLUE OVER YELLOW   BLUE   YELLOW OVER BLUE

FIG.4   YELLOW   RED GLAZE   YELLOW   GREEN GLAZE

COLOR MIXING

Preliminary experiments in the mixing of various colors to determine their potentialities are of definite value to the student.

You may not care to construct color wheels or to paint numerous charts that demonstrate various theories of color. Nevertheless, you should know what occurs when colors are mixed together, when they are placed side by side, or when one color is laid over another.

On the left is a simplified demonstration of basic color mixing. Our problem is an easy one. Using two primary colors, blue and red, we are to make a secondary color, violet. Elementary as this problem is, the novice invariably comes up with a muddy, heavy purple. Knowing that he has chosen the proper primary colors, he immediately attempts to correct the mixture by adding white to lighten the color. This time he finds that he has made it too light, resulting in an anemic shade of lavender. He returns to his red, adds a bit, obtains a red violet, and follows with a hasty addition of blue. After much mixing and stirring of paint he finally arrives at a dull violet. (Figure 1)

A simple way of achieving the desired color is to mix the primaries as in Figure 2. Cut the blue with white as one mixture and cut the red with white for the second mixture. Then, dipping your brush lightly into the first mixture, paint a few strokes of blue into the square. After wiping the brush with a rag, dip the brush into the second mixture and apply a few strokes of red to the square. Do not try to avoid the blue strokes; instead, allow the red to partly overlap some of the previously laid blue. Keep alternating the color strokes, gradually covering the square. If you do not stir the mixture too vigorously, you will get a far more vibrant and true violet.

To sum up, for lively effects in landscape painting do more mixing of the color on your canvas and a minimum amount of stirring on the palette.

Figure 3 shows the handling and effect of one color painted over another.

A square of yellow is painted. Then, while the yellow is still wet, blue is painted over it. The object is not to produce a green, but to show how, through careful manipulation of the brush, a contrasting color can be painted over another without disturbing the wet undercolor. The yellow underneath will, of course, affect the blue slightly, but the result should be far from green. The next example is more difficult. A square of blue is painted and an overpainting of yellow is applied. The deeper undercolor will affect the lighter yellow

more than in the first example. However, if the brush work is handled carefully, the yellow should still predominate.

Use the long flat-haired bristle brush when doing this exercise, as it is less likely to disturb the undercolor. The short-haired bristle brush has a tendency to dig into the paint. Actually, the soft-haired flat sable brushes make for easier painting of one color over another color, but they lack the vigorous stroke of the bristle brush. This painting of one color over the other is of particular benefit in keeping your color from being ordinary and uninteresting. An example would be the painting of a blue sky. A warm ochre or light red could first be painted and then over-painted with blue. The resulting sky would be far more atmospheric than one of an obvious blue.

Figure 4 shows how a glaze of color is affected by an undertone. A square of yellow is painted and allowed to dry. A bit of alizarin crimson is then squeezed into a small paint pan or saucer. Pour some of your copal painting medium into the pan and mix with the alizarin crimson. Stir it thoroughly until the paint is dissolved. The mixture should be of a watery consistency. Then, using a flat sable brush, wash the glaze over the yellow. The first glaze will affect the yellow slightly, turning it toward an orange. The more glazes applied, the stronger the red appears. Luminosity is achieved by applying a series of glazes one over the other until the desired intensity of color is reached, rather than by using one heavier color glaze at the start.

Repeat the same procedure, this time using viridian instead of alizarin crimson over the yellow. When complete, note how much more vibrant the viridian is than if you had painted it directly on a white surface.

In a later chapter details are given of subjects in which glazing can be used effectively. At the start of this chapter I mentioned the cutting of colors with white to arrive at a desired color. This was a specific example of obtaining a certain color and vibrancy without overmixing. I am not implying that white should always be used when mixing colors. Indeed, the reason that so many beginners' paintings have such a washed-out look is the overuse of white paint. I have a vivid recollection of being in a class years ago where one of my fellow student's work always had an anemic, chalky look. The instructor restricted the student's use of white paint to an absolute minimum and further insisted that a touch of yellow ochre be used in the white whenever the latter was to be mixed with another color. Everything the student painted, following this limitation, resulted in a very low key, but the washed-out look was eliminated. Later, when allowed the free use of white paint again, the student had completely overcome any tendency toward chalkiness.

As for the mixing of various colors on the palette, use the knife whenever feasible. Keep in mind that every time you add one color to another, you generally reduce the brilliancy. Therefore, the more colors that are added to a mixture, the greyer the results. Using the knife rather than the brush will prevent the over-mixing of any combination of colors. Constant stirring with a brush will produce a muddy result because the hairs quickly blend the colors. In contrast, the blade of the knife tends to keep the color broken.

When you plan a studio painting and intend to work on it over a period of time, you should consider the drying qualities of the colors you are going to use. Whenever possible, plan to use faster drying colors in the preliminary stages for the underpainting and the slower drying colors for the latter stages. Cracking can be caused by the painting of a fast-drying color over a slow-drying one. In short, follow the housepainter's rule of "fat over lean."

The following colors of our palette are listed according to their relative drying qualities:

MEDIUM FAST
Burnt sienna
Yellow ochre
Oxide of chromiums
Light red
Mars colors

MEDIUM SLOW
Ultramarines

FAST
Raw umber
Burnt umber
Cerulean blue
Cobalt blue
Viridian

SLOW
Ivory black
Cadmiums
Alizarin crimson
Zinc white

A fast-drying color can be mixed with a slow-drying color to help accelerate the drying of the latter. I have recently substituted mars black for ivory black on my palette because of its faster drying qualities and stronger tinting power.

As you mix various colors together, you will note how some pigments have far more tinting strength than others. This is particularly apparent in student's paintings when indian red, light red, or the phthalocynine colors of blue and green are used. They seem to get into all the other paints used and to dominate the over-all color effect. Care must be exercised to control these powerful colors.

The following lists the color of our palette in two groups according to their tinting strength:

Strong Tinting Power
Light red
Chromium oxide green
   (opaque)
Phthalocyanide blue
Phthalocyanide green
The mars colors

Average Tinting Power
French ultramarine
Alizarin crimson
Burnt sienna
Cerulean blue
Ivory black
Raw umber
Burnt umber
Cadmium yellow
Cadmium red
Cadmium orange
Yellow ochre
Raw sienna

PICTORIAL PRELIMINARIES

The illustration on this page shows how a simple pencil sketch, rendered from nature, is of far more value to the painter than is a photograph. Both were made from the same position. Note how the camera has flattened the subject, particularly the road, and exaggerated the distance of the receding planes.

Even the most fragmentary sketch has more artistic value. As an authoritative note, it can form the basis for a future painting far better than the sharpest of photographs. Along with the distortion of perspective, the very sharpness of the photograph defeats the novice, for he becomes confused by too many cold details.

It is true that many illustrators today use the photograph, but it must be remembered that they are skillful draftsmen who are familiar with the limitations of a photograph and use it accordingly. When time is limited, the photograph can serve to gather details together, such as the rigging on a boat and historic buildings where every window must be accounted for, or even to aid in recalling to mind the scene as it was when the sketch was made.

I painted the subject in my studio, using the sketch and photograph above for reference. Note the inclusion of a figure to relieve the montonous area of the road.

It is obvious that the sketch contributed far more to the realization of the subject than could any photograph.

21

SUBJECT MATTER

Very often the student spends a great deal of time looking for a subject to paint. He may, for example, walk for hours along a country road, waiting for an ideal scene to appear just beyond the next turn. In all probability he has unwittingly passed up several perfectly good subjects. If he had devoted some time to observance of possible subjects from different angles and had penciled a few quick compositional roughs, he would have saved a good deal of time and energy.

This search for the picturesque or ready-made landscape, comprising ideal color, composition, and subject matter, often actually results in an unexciting, dull picture.

There is a school of painting today, steadily gaining in popularity, whose followers deliberately avoid doing the obviously popular subjects. The base of the trunk of a tree, a section of the side of a barn, an aged door, a lone steeple against the sky — such are the subjects, all apparently simple, that are used as complete compositions by the painters of this school. But it is their very simplicity that is most deceiving. It takes deep probing, restraint, highly developed skill, and technical knowledge, let alone artistry, to do these subjects convincingly.

All of us go through periods of searching for various subject material to help interpret the particular phase of art we are interested in at the time.

An example of a rather unusual subject, one that affords a wealth of color and textural material,

for which I was searching, is reproduced here. The painting is of a town's dumping grounds. The grey ashes from the burnt refuse were piled high. Objects that could not burn, such as springs from discarded mattresses, hooples from barrels, and cans, were a rusty red. Ocherish wooden packing cases, partly blackened, and soddy brown cardboard cartons whose burning had been temporarily postponed by rainfall — formed the base. A discarded Christmas tree made an excellent note with clinging tinsel contributing its share of color. And, in the midst of all this debris, sunflowers were blooming!

I thought that the title, "Love's Labor's Lost," was most appropriate.

REVERSING PROPORTION TO VARY THE COMPOSITION

There is a tendency for students to paint every landscape on a horizontal canvas. While undoubtedly most scenes lend themselves more readily to horizontal compositions, an occasional painting of the subject vertically will often result in a more interesting canvas.

Below is a composition placed in the usual horizon-

tal position. Alongside is the same subject planned to a vertical composition.

You will find that this switching of proportion will often enliven an otherwise ordinary composition.

22

GUIDING THE SPECTATOR'S INTEREST

There are several pictorial devices that may be employed to guide and control the spectator's interest. Below are compositions illustrating some of the methods.

The first illustration is an extreme example of guiding the viewer to the lower left center of the composition. The railroad tracks, the cloud formation, the telegraph poles, and the hillside light and shadows all combine to lead the eye to this spot.

The second illustration, in which the direction of line is to the farmhouse and barns, is a bit more subtle; the road, the walking figure, the rows of vegetables, the leafless tree, the fence and post — all help focus attention on the buildings. Once the eye reaches that point, the surrounding dark trees hold the spectator's interest.

The third and fourth illustrations, at the bottom of the page, show how an area can be made to appear larger or smaller. If you eliminate the trees, both pictures are the same. By enlarging the trees in the immediate foreground, the background recedes and becomes less imposing. By reversing the process and making the trees smaller, the background immediately becomes more majestic and important.

As you develop your sketches into studio pictures, you will discover various devices that will minimize features you wish to subdue and that will enhance those which are to be the center of interest.

The use of color will, of course, be of the greatest importance in controlling the eye as well as the emotion of the viewer.

STRENGTHENING THE DESIGN

Another approach to painting a subject and strengthening its design is to reduce all the pictorial elements to simple, but significant, shapes.

Before applying any pigment to the canvas, spend some time in observing the scene and determining which elements are essential and which are unnecessary. Begin working, omitting all superfluous details and painting only the important masses, reducing them to their basic shapes. This approach enables you to concentrate on strengthening the basic design, with all the distracting frills removed (see Figure 1). After the important shapes have been painted in a flat poster-like color, you can then resume portraying the surface quality of the subject to whatever degree of finish desired (see Figure 2). This method is most helpful to the painter who is inclined to put in too many unessential details, especially at the beginning of a painting.

A reversal of this process will also prove interesting, as well as stimulating. A representational painting is made on the spot that is no more than a literal rendering of the scene before you (see Figure 3). Later, in the studio, using the painting as a guide, another can be made, reducing all the elements to their most abstract shapes (see Figure 4).

In my studio I frequently work a semi-abstract composition into a more representational finished painting.

I assemble before me notes that may consist of anything from penciled notations to an on-the-spot watercolor sketch of the subject.

Using charcoal, I proceed to compose directly on my canvas, reducing all of the contributing notes and sketches to a semi-abstract design. Then, spraying the canvas with fixatif, I redraw the design into a more realistic interpretation, using a brush and a single color.

The realism may be developed still further, if desired, as color is applied to the canvas.

VARYING THE POINT OF VIEW

It is surprising how seldom the student really strives to discover the various compositions that can be found in a single subject. Below are four illustrations that are examples of how, simply by turning the head or by moving a short distance from the original point of view, a new interpretation can be given to the same subject.

Figure 1 is the first composition. Figure 2 is arrived at simply by walking a bit forward and about 20 feet to the right of the view shown in Figure 1.

In Figure 3 the subject is painted from the base of the hill. By going half way up the hill, a close view enabled me to concentrate on the houses as a center of interest. The bay that was in the distance comes into view now and is used as a background for the houses. To improve the composition, I transposed the tree and the telegraph poles. These are but a few of the possible compositions that can be obtained by simply shifting one's point of view.

The view finder, a time-tested device, is of great aid to the student in selecting and arranging his composition. A piece of cardboard, preferably black, is trimmed to approximately 6 inches by 8 inches. A 3-inch by 4-inch opening is cut in the center of this area. By holding the card a short distance away from the eye, you can concentrate on the subject through the opening. Maneuver the card up and down or from side to side to arrive at a pleasing arrangement.

The average sketching box provides for 12-inch by 16-inch panels. The 3-inch by 4-inch opening is in the same proportion, thus facilitating the transposition of the subject to the panel.

Most students eventually discard this device as they overcome their initial bewilderment in attempting to select the amount of subject matter to include in the composition. However, it will be surprising how often it can be used when doing architectural subjects in which, because artistic liberties must be kept at a minimum, the composition is necessarily limited.

ENLARGING A SKETCH

While painters employ different methods of enlarging a sketch, probably one of the simplest is to use a sheet of glass. It is necessary that the glass be large enough to cover the entire area of the original sketch.

Assuming the sketch is on a 12-inch by 16-inch panel, proceed to rule in horizontal and vertical lines placed two inches apart (see Figure 1).

Any grease or china marking pencil will adhere to the glass surface. Then, on a canvas 24 inches by 32 inches, rule the lines in the same manner four inches apart.

By placing the ruled glass pane over the sketch, the marked squares immediately act as a guide in transferring the approximate areas to the large canvas (see Figure 2).

A simple example of a two-to-one proportion has been illustrated. Any variations of this formula can easily be worked out. Frequently it may be desirable to change certain areas of the sketch as it is being enlarged. The ruled glass method will still be feasible in giving the general proportions, thus eliminating excessive preliminary penciling or charcoal drawing on the canvas.

FIGURE 1

FIGURE 2

Another use for the glass in spotting figures

It is always a problem to place a figure exactly where it will be in harmony with the rest of the composition.

One way to determine the right area is to place a sheet of glass over the entire painting. Then, using oil paint on the glass, spot the figure in the most likely position. The painter can then clearly see the relation of the figure to the composition of the rest of the painting, visible through the glass. If the position is not satisfactory, wipe the figure off with a rag dipped in turpentine and repaint it in another area until you obtain a satisfactory composition.

Cloud shapes, houses, and the like, along with vital color notes, can also be previewed the same way. Once you hit on a satisfactory arrangement, remove the glass and paint the object directly on the canvas. The location of the figure in Figure 3 was determined by this method.

THE APPROACH TO LANDSCAPE PAINTING

Of all mediums, oil painting is by far the most popular for study purposes. Even. if you intend to work eventually in watercolor, pastel, or any other medium, painting in oil is the most flexible method of study if you want to know just what takes place in nature and to interpret your findings pictorially. You will note that in all of the step-by-step demonstrations in this book, a drawing or some roughly indicated construction lines precede the actual painting of each subject. The degree of drawing necessary depends upon two factors: the complexity of the subject and the ability of the student to grasp the subject.

The subjects illustrated below show three types of approach.

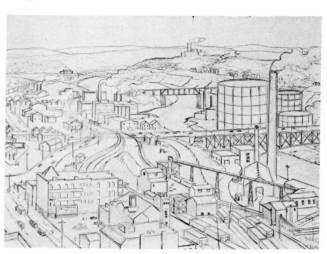

1. If the subject is complicated, make a detailed drawing, preferably with charcoal. Spray the drawing with fixatif or dust it off lightly, allowing a faint impression to remain. Then, with a fine brush and a single color, redraw to the degree you wish.

2. If the subject is fairly simple and the light and dark pattern already clearly defined by nature's lighting, you can often dispense with the preliminary drawing. Then, with just roughly indicated construction lines, you can immediately start to lay in tonal arrangement, using just one color.

3. When a fleeting effect is to be captured, omit the preliminary drawing or tonal lay-in. Apply the color directly, as quickly as possible, using plenty of medium to facilitate handling of the paint.

ABOUT THE DEMONSTRATIONS THAT FOLLOW

In all of the following demonstrations a drawing or roughly indicated composition precedes the painting. There can be no doubt that if you first make a detailed drawing on the canvas, you gain confidence in the knowledge that you have laid a sound foundation. However, as the actual painting progresses, it is not necessary that this drawing be rigidly adhered to. Simplify areas and, in some instances, eliminate early details and supply new ones. The main purpose of the drawing is to establish boundaries for the subsequent laying in of the tonal values.

The color plate on the opposite page shows the steps that are followed from the drawing to the finished painting of an average subject.

After the charcoal drawing has been made, spray it with fixatif or dust it off lightly with a rag, allowing just a faint impression to remain as a guide. Using ultramarine blue and a small brush, redraw the subject and make any changes that will strengthen the design. Follow with a lay-in of the same blue, indicating the distribution of the light and dark areas. This application of a single color, which hereafter I will refer to as a monochromatic lay-in, has several advantages. It is an excellent way to bridge the abrupt change from the outlined drawing to the application of full color. It immediately determines the pattern of the picture by the distribution of the light and dark areas. (The light areas are the untouched portions of the white canvas.) It also gives you a chance to reconstruct or redesign any areas before a mass of unwieldy paint has accumulated on the canvas. You can further reduce the unwieldy paint by using little or no medium and rubbing the paint on the canvas in a dry-brush manner.

Another frequent advantage of this approach occurs when a subject, although attractive in outline, seems to lose something when full color is applied directly. The monochromatic lay-in affords you a chance to make any readjustment necessary between line and mass before the color is applied. The next step shows the start in the using of color. The color is applied only to the dark areas, with the white of the canvas continuing to represent the light area. It is still preferable to use no medium, or at least only very little if it is necessary to make the paint easier to handle. After you paint the dark areas, paint the light passages in the same way. At this stage you have covered the entire canvas, with the exception of the white areas of the clouds and the light side of the house. Apply a brush stroke of pure white paint where the light side of the house meets the shadowed side, and thus establish the highest light.

Do not, while you are covering the canvas, try too hard to keep within the blue outline. An undesirable tightness often results. Students often become bewildered when they lose an outline too quickly. In attempting to regain some semblance of the originally intended picture, they overload the canvas with paint that fast turns into a muddy mass of color. If this happens to you, and you have applied the paint in the thin manner described, you can easily go back and reconstruct the original blue outline.

The blue will not be disturbing visually at this stage, as it is a color that is harmonious to the landscape. Continue, now applying the paint in a more solid manner, especially in the light areas. Medium can be used if desired. Try to keep the same degree of completeness over the entire canvas. The blue outline gradually disappears as the painting progresses and is finished.

To sum up, this procedure serves four definite purposes:
1. It establishes a solid foundation or "scaffolding" for painting.
2. It immediately determines the pattern of light and dark.
3. It affords you an opportunity to make any readjustment necessary between line and mass *before* the problem of color is encountered.
4. It lessens the chances that, because of the accumulation of too much paint, you will lose control of the painting.

All of the subjects demonstrated can be painted without waiting for a drying interval between stages, with the following exceptions. The demonstration of casein as an underpainting and the descriptions of glazing and scumbling technique do require a drying period. Information on the length of the period is given in the chapters covering those subjects. However, it should be noted that certain areas of a painting can be handled with greater technical facility when surrounding areas are dry. Or, again, a dried surface may be desirable in order to obtain certain effects by later painting. I shall mention this point whenever appropriate during the demonstrations in this book.

If, in the course of working, you put a painting aside and it is dry to the touch when you take it up again, you can apply a coat of retouch varnish to it. This varnish will help restore color that has sunk into the canvas and dried dull. It will also form a better adhering bond for the subsequent painting. You can spray the varnish on with an atomizer or use a soft varnishing brush. In either case, apply only a light coating.

THE HOUSE ON THE HILL

Just as Motif #1 is famous to all the artists who have visited Rockport, Massachusetts, so the House on the Hill can be considered the Universal Motif. A simple subject, it can be found everywhere and makes an ideal composition for the first demonstration.

I earnestly recommend that you carry, along with your paint box, a small sketch pad. It is invaluable for an important purpose: the making of preliminary pencil notes to help you plan and select the composition that you wish to paint. The notes can be very simple, merely showing the main lines of the composition, or they can be carried further by indicating light and shade as well. It is the combination of your knowledge and the subject's complexity that decides how much preliminary work you must do. One thing is certain: your first pencil note generally will be of the most obvious composition. Not until you attempt several rough compositions will you achieve a more interesting arrangement.

As mentioned in the introduction, the illustrations in this how-to-do-it book are literal interpretations so designed that the point I am trying to make may be more quickly grasped. However, in your own studies you should make every effort to keep your compositions from becoming ordinary.

Above: a page from an 11" x 15" sketch pad, showing the rough composition made preparatory to the painting.

STEP 1. *First sketch the subject with charcoal, indicating the main lines of the composition. Next, spray on fixatif to keep the drawing from smearing, or lightly dust off the charcoal with a rag, retaining only a faint impression of the subject. Then, using french ultramarine, preferably with little or no medium, strengthen the outline. Do not apply the paint heavily; instead, employ a dry-brush technique. The omission of the medium helps to achieve this effect.*

STEP 2. *Now paint the dark or shaded areas, still using only french ultramarine. The paint is applied with a bristle brush, rubbing the pigment into the tooth of the canvas. Do not shorten the brush strokes in order to hold the painting to the edge of the outline. Attempt, rather, to achieve a sketchy or free effect, allowing the edges to blur. If you feel that too much of the original outline is lost, you can redraw it with french ultramarine before starting the next step.*

STEP 3. *Still using a dry-brush technique, paint the same dark areas in full color. Try to avoid the use of too much white paint. Depend upon the rubbing-in or dry-brush technique to lighten or darken the colors by varying the amount of paint used and the pressure applied. Bits of the white canvas should be breaking through the thinly-rubbed dark areas if the procedure has been followed correctly. At the conclusion of this step all of the dark color areas have been covered, with the unpainted part of the canvas representing the light areas.*

STEP 4. *By checking the painting at this stage, you will have a general idea of just how the picture is shaping up. If too much paint has accumulated in any one spot, scrape it off with the palette knife. In any of the following demonstrations do not hesitate to scrape off the paint if it has become objectionably heavy or poor in color. If you are satisfied with the general over-all effect, you can now repaint the areas in a more solid manner. (Refer to the color plate for the color scheme.) At the finish of this step the sky is still untouched with solid paint. A few brush strokes are made on the light side of the house and at the base of the path to establish the correct tone and color, preparatory to the painting of the light areas.*

STEP 5. *The light area of the house is now painted, followed by the path leading to the house. The painting of the sky is then accomplished, with the color first laid in with a flat bristle brush and smoothed down with a flat sable brush. Paint the broken warm color at the base of the hill, and shape the shadows in the road.*

The colors used for "The House on the Hill" were as follows: french ultramarine was used for the sky with viridian added to it as it neared the house; the shadow side of the house was a combination of light red, french ultramarine, and a touch of yellow ochre; the rooftops were burnt sienna with a touch of cadmium yellow light; yellow ochre was used for the chimneys, the windows, and the road; the distant rooftops were alizarin crimson; french ultramarine was added for the shadow areas of the house; viridian, with cadmium yellow light added as it reached the base, was added for the hill.

PAINTING DIRECTLY IN COLOR

In contrast to the method I described before, of first doing a drawing and a monochromatic toning-in, is the painting of the subject directly in full color.

Instead of isolating each problem progressively, we now have to do the drawing and establish tone and color at the same time we do the composition. However, the charm and spontaneity that this "all-in-one" approach brings to a painting is most rewarding. In this demonstration our chief concern is to maintain control of the canvas from start to finish.

In order to simplify the problem, select a subject that has clearly defined patterns of both color and objects. This is important because in working directly we have dispensed with the usual preliminaries. Take the additional precaution of having plenty of paint rags on hand, along with a separate cup of turpentine to keep the brushes clean at all times. Use varnish in the medium to give a "pull" to the brush and to facilitate the handling of the paint. This is especially helpful when painting one color over the other. A good medium will be one made up of one third turpentine, one third linseed oil, and the remaining third copal oil varnish. The commercially prepared copal painting medium is excellent.

In direct painting, spend little time in trying to match nature's colors on your palette. Rather, attempt to put the color on the canvas as soon as possible, placing one color against another and then adjusting their relation to each other. In such a manner the canvas is gradually covered (see top color plate on page 36). From this stage to the end, check the canvas, modifying or strengthening color where necessary, correcting values, simplifying, and finally adding whatever details you feel are needed.

STEP 1. *The usual charcoal preliminary drawing is omitted. Using french ultramarine, a few construction lines are indicated to show the general arrangement of the subject. The shadow side of the red house is painted, matching nature's color as closely as possible. This is followed by the painting of the shaded areas of the rest of the buildings. With the painting of the water, a fairly comprehensive preview is obtained of the pattern of the picture. Unlike our previous demonstration, where the use of medium was restricted until the final stages, here medium is used from the start to the finish.*

STEP 2. *The pattern is more clearly defined as the rest of the dark areas are painted. Keep the handling free, making no attempt to be conscious of the brush, concentrating only on color. Use enough medium so that the canvas receives the paint easily. At the conclusion of this step the over-all effect should be one of sketchiness, with the canvas showing through in many spots of the shaded areas.*

STEP 3. *The sky is now painted, followed by the application of color to the light areas of the buildings and the various objects. The untouched surface of the canvas is allowed to remain, to represent the light area of the snow. The completion of this step is shown in full color on the following page.*

The white areas representing the snow are the original canvas in Step 3 above. The final stage shown below is the gradual tightening up of the entire painting, resulting in a more solidly painted picture. The edges of the various objects are sharpened when the light areas meet the dark. The snow-covered areas are now painted with a full brush, imparting an impasto effect. The picture is completed with the painting of details. In a final checking up of the painting the sea gulls were added to give a feeling of life to the subject.

THE AUTUMN SCENE

In the chapter on color I said that the autumn season possessed such a variety of colors that restraint had to be used when transposing them to your canvas. We learned that brilliant color was not achieved by the use of raw color alone but that the more subtle greys had to be sought to bring out or enhance the color.

It is advisable for the novice to select a fairly simple subject when painting the autumn scene. Do not permit too many trees and clusters of vari-colored foliage to dominate your composition. Rather, select a scene in open country, using a single tree and farmhouse as an initial subject.

You can attempt more ambitious canvases after you have become familiar with autumn landscapes and have learned to resist the riot of color by simplifying and playing up the various greys.

On the right are three preliminary versions of the same subject.

The top composition is an ordinary interpretation too frequently acceptable to the student. No attempt has been made to rearrange any of the elements into a more exciting composition. The foreground, middleground, and background are evenly divided, and the general effect is one of monotony. By allowing part of the tree to go beyond the canvas, rearranging the group of buildings, and stressing the rolling land, the middle example immediately becomes more interesting.

Noting how the composition was improved, a third was started. If cropping part of the tree was an aid to the second composition, why not be a bit more daring and have it run out of the base of the canvas as well as the top and side? And to add more impact to the feeling of rolling hills, we exaggerate the swelling lines to an even greater degree.

When we compare the first composition with the last, we discover that we can develop a much more interesting picture by emphasizing certain elements and subduing others. As in most of life's endeavors, experimentation and thought lead to a better result.

Instead of roughing in various arrangements directly on canvas, necessitating the removal of the previous drawing each time a new composition is sought, use the sketch book method as suggested in the demonstration, "The House on the Hill."

STEP 1. *Having decided upon the composition, outline the subject in french ultramarine. Apply the paint thinly in a dry-brush manner, eliminating medium if necessary. Do not be concerned yet about showing too much detail. Indicate the rolling hill in the foreground by rubbing the ultramarine lightly over the canvas. Try to achieve a looseness in the handling of the brush and avoid a tight drawing.*

STEP 2. *Still using only the french ultramarine, quickly rub in a tone over the large tree in the foreground. This roughly establishes the range from the principle dark area to the white of the canvas. This will suffice for the monochromatic lay-in, as we are anxious to start using full color.*

STEP 3. *Some burnt umber is painted thinly, using as little medium as possible, over the french ultramarine of the large tree. Allow the umber to mix freely with the ultramarine. Lighten the umber with yellow ochre and paint the shadow side of the barns. Using these same two colors, add a touch of ultramarine and white and mix a grey. Use this mixture for the dark areas of the white houses and silo. Establish the very darkest note in the subject by mixing french ultramarine, alizarin crimson, and viridian and paint the two holes in the tree. Incidentally, remember this mixture whenever you wish to obtain an even more intense dark than black paint. The step is concluded with a thin rub-in of cadmium red and yellow to roughly indicate the bushes in the foreground.*

38

STEP 4. *The distant foliage is painted with alizarin crimson with a touch of french ultramarine to give it a more violet cast. Some viridian is brushed in at the base with no attempt to model the forms. The fields are given a toning of yellow ochre followed by the painting of the distant blue mountain. Do not attempt to paint around the trees at the right of the middleground; it can be redrawn and painted in later.*

STEP 5. *Paint the sky in the greyed color so typical of late autumn. Yellow ochre, french ultramarine, and just a touch of ivory black will give you the effect. Paint right over the branches of the large tree; then, when the sky is completed, repaint the branches. Paint the remaining areas of the fields and the light areas of the buildings, referring to the color plate on page 41 for color. With the repainting of the trees on the extreme right your entire canvas should be covered with paint.*

STEP 6. *Now paint all the details. The bushes in the foreground are given more solidity by touches of cadmium red, yellow, and orange, applied with a painting knife. The distant foliage is reshaped and painted in a more solid manner. The trees are refined and the windows of the house sharpened. (In checking up the over-all effect, I felt that the subject could be improved pictorially by extending a branch of the large tree downward so that it crossed the front of the white house.) The painting is completed by painting fence posts, some lines to indicate the wooden texture of the barns, and the leaves on the large tree. To give the subject a note of interest, add a figure walking along the road.*

The rendering of the detailed bark of the large tree is illustrated here. A round sable brush that comes to a fine point is used for this subject. The same brush is used to suggest the small branches of the bushes in the foreground and the distant foliage.

THE WATERFRONT

A scene in which the main object of interest is not stationary always presents difficulties to the painter.

The ever popular boat picture is typical of a fascinating subject that can become most irritating because the main object, the boat, moves about while you are trying to put it on canvas.

Such experiences soon teach you that you must paint rapidly if you would capture moving objects or fleeting effects. There are several ways that you can speed up the application of paint from palette to canvas.

One method is to reduce the natural pull or resistance of oil paint on canvas by cutting the paint to an almost watery consistency with turpentine, and to work on a smoother canvas. A monochromatic composition is then quickly painted; this will resemble a watercolor more than an oil. Once you have achieved a satisfactory arrangement, you can proceed to concentrate on the color.

Again, if you are striving for an effect of fleeting color, you can omit the monochromatic stage and paint directly with the cut pigment.

While the result will be little more than a staining of the canvas, it will provide enough of a color note to permit you to proceed directly with the use of solid paint.

Another method — one that is more successful with the smaller canvas panels — is to first wipe the entire surface with a rag that has been dipped in the painting medium being used (preferably linseed oil), and then paint swiftly with color. The smooth, oily base offers no resistance to the application of the paint and facilitates the brush work (see Figure 1).

One more aid in doing quick sketches, particularly in capturing color effect, is to cover the entire

FIGURE 1

white canvas panel with a flat tone of paint that has been cut with turpentine. You can use any color, but preferably one of a warm tone, that is harmonious with the color scheme.

This tone can be applied with a rag dipped in turpentine; it will dry very quickly. You may then paint the subject directly in color. Any portions left untouched will be in keeping with the general over-all effect. With an untoned base, the original white canvas breaking through would be a disturbing note. This method is a variation of the imprimatura method that is described fully in a later chapter.

In this demonstration, working on a smooth canvas, I used only turpentine for the monochromatic lay-in. Although the large boat remained fairly stationary, the two smaller boats in the lower right of the canvas were constantly moving back and forth. When they assumed a position that seemed most pleasing to the rest of the composition, I quickly sketched them in. I followed the same procedure in the placing of the rowboat containing the two men.

The canvas which has been given a quick warm toning is shown on the left.
The same canvas after the sketch has been completed can be seen on the right.

STEP 1. *Omit the preliminary charcoal drawing so that you can capture the moving objects as soon as possible. Quickly sketch in the composition with french ultramarine cut with turpentine.*

STEP 2. *Establish the tones with the same color, cutting the paint with still more turpentine in order to obtain a watercolor effect. The paint should be thin enough for the outline to show through.*

STEP 3. *Begin the application of color, using copal painting medium. Paint the large boat first, as it dominates the composition, and then paint the smaller boats. The white boat, with the seated figure, and its reflection are left unpainted, leaving the white of the canvas to represent the color at this stage. Some of the dark is indicated at the back of the figure to fix its position.*

STEP 4. *Now paint the sky, letting the white of the canvas indicate the shape of the clouds. The water, being vitally affected by the color of the sky, follows. Use plenty of medium in order to obtain a fluid quality. This stage is concluded by painting the background in its approximate color.*

STEP 5. *Continue by painting the boathouse and the supporting piers. The figures in the rowboat are then rendered and sharpened by silhouetting them against the water, which is repainted in a higher key to intensify the glare.*

STEP 6. *The clouds, which you have indicated by leaving the canvas white, are now painted and reshaped to help the design. Follow with the painting of the nets, using a loaded brush to suggest their texture. All of the light areas are then painted in a solid manner. Paint a warmer tone into the lower portion of the boathouse where it is affected by the warm reflected light from the top of the dock. The side of the large vessel is also intensified by a warm light in contrast to the cooler color of the piers. The white boat, which had been represented by leaving the canvas bare, is now painted. As this is accomplished, the boat becomes more brilliant because the original white key of the canvas was lower than the now built-up white paint.*

45

While this demonstration shows the approach to the painting of moving objects on-the-spot, additional work can be done upon returning to the studio. Any refinements you wish to make, as well as further building up of the light areas, can be accomplished at that time.

After the painting is dry to the touch, give it a coat of retouch varnish. The broken texture of the nets can be emphasized by omitting any medium and dragging the color over the previously painted area in a dry-brush manner. In this way you can show details more easily and repaint highlights more crisply than if you tried to work into a wet surface on the spot.

This demonstration also serves as an example of what can happen when an area is finally painted in a key lighter and higher than the original white of the base canvas, as in the case of the white boat. Care must be exercised that the objects enveloping this white area are not painted too dark in the earlier stages. Make allowance for the fact that the darks will look much darker when the light object they are surrounding is eventually painted in a higher key.

This readjustment of values will be a constant problem, but it is all part of creating a picture. However, refrain from too much repainting, otherwise you may end up with an overpainted, unpleasant surface.

Shown at the left is the use of the rigger brush in delineating a fine line. It is not gripped by the ferrule, but held loosely below the center of the wooden handle.

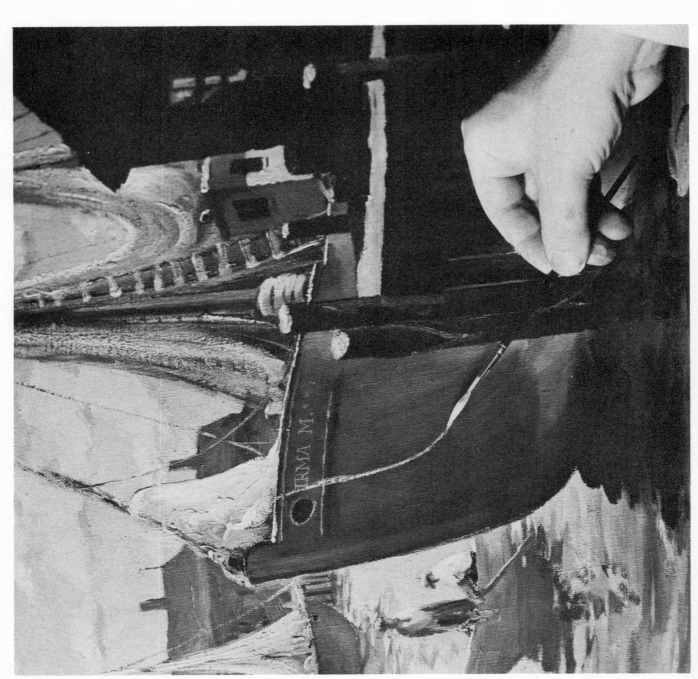

46

SUMMER YARD

Summer, the most popular season for outdoor painting, offers many opportunities to study the effects created by sunlight.

An endless, glaring green — that is the impression you get when you first view a sunlit landscape. It is not until after you have made several studies that you realize how varied and subtle are the colors which compose the green effect. You will then avoid the obvious greens by using combinations of siennas mixed with french ultramarine, and yellow and orange cadmiums with cobalt blue. Vary these combinations by alternating the cobalt blue with the siennas and the ultramarine with the cadmiums. Viridian and cadmium yellow light will produce a bright green that, in turn, can be subdued with a touch of alizarin crimson.

The glaring effect of brilliant light striking the edges of objects in the landscape (such as the head and shoulders of a figure or along the top of foliage and fence posts) can be achieved by loading paint on these edges. This heavy application of paint conveys the impression of light, in contrast to the shadow areas which are painted more thinly.

Instead of using a brush, you can load the highlights with the tip of your painting knife, which gives a crisper and more decisive edge than does a brush. The chapter on palette knife painting gives further details on combining the use of the knife with the brush in order to vary the painted surface.

The subject chosen for this demonstration is an excellent one for studying sunlight and its effects upon various surfaces. As shadows are such a vital foil in creating the effect of light, care should be taken in selecting the time of day to paint the sunny scene.

The following subject was painted in late afternoon. The same motif viewed at midnoon was not nearly as attractive as later, when the shadows started to lengthen.

The effect of glaring sunlight can often be heightened by slightly lowering the value or intensifying the blue of the sky surrounding the object.

STEP 1. *The drawing is made and yellow ochre is used to strengthen the outline.*

48

STEP 2. *Paint the subject directly in the approximate colors of nature, using enough medium to reduce the paint to a thin consistency. No white paint is used, so at the conclusion of this step the color resembles a stain rather than solid paint. The original yellow ochre can still be seen through the first color lay-in.*

STEP 3. *Paint the dark area of the open barn door with a mixture of alizarin crimson, french ultramarine, and viridian. This establishes the deepest tone in the dark area. The painting of the barn and fence follows, and the shadows cast from these objects are strengthened. Add a bit of cadmium orange where a warmer tone is desired, as in the over-hanging roof of the barn and in the cast shadow. Once you have painted the dark areas, you will note that the original outline starts to disappear. This loss is proper, for we are now thinking in terms of color. The outline has served its purpose, which was to define the boundaries of the subsequent application of color.*

STEP 4. *Now paint the light areas, applying the paint in a manner heavier than when you painted the darks. The feeling of sunlight is conveyed more convincingly when the light is painted with heavier paint in a more solid manner. In turn the shaded areas are more transparent, as they should be, when painted thinly. Heighten the effect of sunlight by accenting, with a more vivid color, the edges of the lighted areas where they meet the cast shadows. Introduce a red subtle glow at the base of the barn where the warm ground reflects this area. The over-all impression of the completed painting should be one of warm color. While shadowed areas are generally cool, in this subject the warm earth, combined with strong reflecting sunlight, tends to make the shadows much warmer.*

The glare of sunlight is conveyed by applying the paint along the edge of the shrubbery in an impasto manner. Note how the brush is held below the ferrule and the heavy paint is loaded on the tip of the brush. A similar effect can be achieved with the painting knife; however, the brush affords easier control in placing the paint.

THE STREET SCENE

The street scene has always been a source of fascinating subject material for the artist. Such paintings become a record of the times — of how people lived, their dress, the mode of transportation, etc.

Just as every city or town possesses a character of its own, so each street, too, has an individual personality. It is certainly a most accessible subject for the painter. Almost every exhibition includes many paintings of this timely subject as observed in the various seasons. Snow, rain, sunshine — all the elements contribute to keep your interpretation from becoming monotonous.

I have always been interested in the painting of street scenes. Having for many years resided in the same city, I have accumulated a collection of paintings that will serve as a historic record of the community.

One way of painting a street scene is to liken the view before you to a stage setting. I have chosen such an approach for this demonstration. The sidewalks and houses on either side of the street become the wings. The street running parallel to the viewer is about 40 feet back.

The distance between this street and the extreme background (the back drop) can be divided into

THE STAGE SETTING

a series of areas, each representing a certain amount of space. When you paint the street scene, get this feeling of depth or space in your canvas.

Just as a stage designer creates the illusion of perspective, so do we—and we have the advantage of being able to use *true* vanishing points. The people become actors, and the automobile, street lamps, and signs are props to be placed by you in positions which will best promote the over-all effect.

STEP 1. *After roughly indicating a composition, using charcoal for the drawing, a fairly comprehensive monochromatic toning-in is made, using french ultramarine.*

STEP 2. *Painting directly in color, the houses on either side of the street are started. These are to be the wings of our stage setting.*

STEP 3. *As the painting progresses, the stage setting becomes more apparent. We now have developed the wings and floor of the stage. As in all of the previous demonstrations, details are kept at a minimum until the entire canvas is covered with paint.*

STEP 4. *The row of houses directly in back of the wings becomes a flat between our wings and the backdrop. In your painting try to convey the approximate distance this row of houses would be from you (the spectator).*

STEP 5. *Another flat is developed as the painting of the railroad trains and prominent mining areas is accomplished.*

As a means of stressing the feeling of space between the wings and the row of houses, the area directly behind the left wing is "haloed." This is accomplished by lightening and blurring the edge of the background area where it meets the foremost object. Restraint should be exercised so that this does not look too obvious.

STEP 6. As the sky and distant hills are painted, our stage setting is complete with background. You can now concentrate on doing the details that take place in the areas, starting with the foreground. Try not to lose the feeling of space or depth between each step.

Shown here is an example of using the knife to achieve the texture of wires. It would be most difficult to paint the wires as finely as the knife could depict them. Extreme care must be taken in order not to cut too deeply, especially when performing this action on a dry surface.

THE INDUSTRIAL SCENE

Use of a limited palette of colors

For this demonstration I have chosen a subject which lends itself to painting with a limited number of colors. The simplest method of obtaining a harmonious effect in painting is to use as few colors as necessary.

It is surprising how many rich, effective colors you can achieve by employing variations of the three primary colors — red, yellow and blue. An excellent illustration of that fact is to make a painting limiting your palette to light red, yellow ochre, and french ultramarine blue. White is needed, of course, and a small amount of black can further help neutralize the colors named, especially the blue.

The subject matter to be painted with such a palette must necessarily be carefully selected. Flowers would hardly be ideal, nor any vivid, high-keyed subject. Choose, rather, more earthy material, such as can be interpreted best in a low key. One subject ideally suitable for the limited palette is the industrial scene.

Reproduced above at the right is such a subject. The only colors used were raw sienna, indian red, and cobalt blue, along with white and black. A grey day was chosen, to allow a low-keyed atmosphere to prevail over the entire scene. All of the objects were reduced to silhouettes whenever possible as an aid in retaining the low-keyed aspect. Both the sunlight breaking through the overcast clouds and the light smoke were designed to enhance these silhouettes.

In turn, the white posts and white buildings gave a sharp contrasting note to the over-all low key of the rest of the painting.

Try to discover as many combinations of red, yellow, and blue that you can without using the three accepted primaries. After completing a limited palette painting, you can carry these experiments further by introducing a foreign color as a contrasting note.

For example: you have completed a low-keyed woodland subject. In a vital spot, say along a narrow path near the center of the picture, insert a small figure. Paint this figure clothed in a bright pink blouse or dress. You will see immediately how this foreign note "sings" out against the limited and low-keyed color of the rest of the canvas.

STEP 1. *Compose the subject on the canvas with charcoal. Then redraw it, using cobalt blue. As the subject contains quite some detail, a small, pointed brush is used to obtain a sharply defined line.*

STEP 2. *Using our limited palette of colors — cobalt blue, indian red, and raw sienna and at this stage a little white — the canvas is quickly covered. Plenty of medium is used to cut the paint to an almost watercolor consistency. An increased amount of turpentine has been added as a fast-drying aid. At this stage the canvas should resemble a washed-out version of the color plate on page 61.*

STEP 3. *Still using only the colors mentioned above, plus an occasional touch of black, the canvas is repainted in a solid manner. As you work with this limited palette, you will be surprised at the variety of colors that can be obtained. At the same time the over-all effect will always be harmonious.*

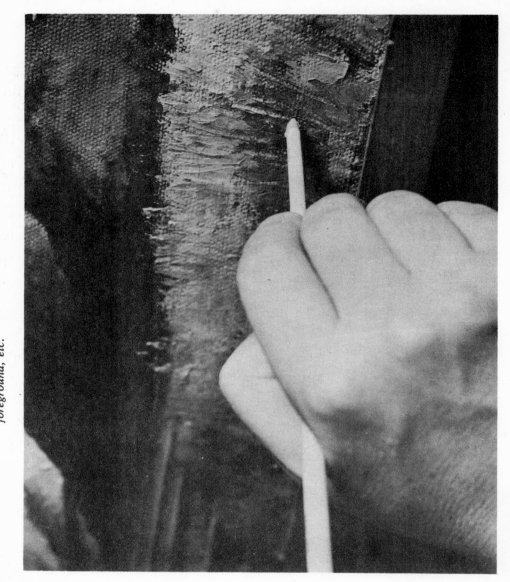

On the left is seen the use of a ruler as a prop or improvised maulstick, to act as a steadying guide in the painting of a straight line.

Below is demonstrated the use of the wooden end of the brush to break the layer of wet paint, imparting the texture of grass, broken foreground, etc.

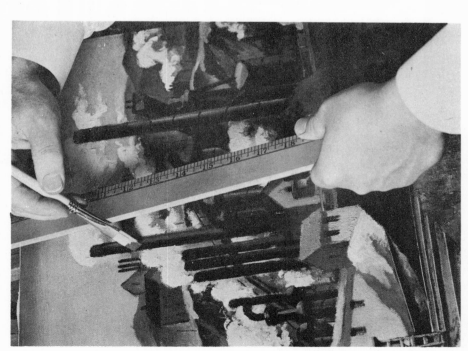

PAINTING A NOCTURNE

Less painted than any other subject by the landscape artist is the night scene. A visit to any exhibition, whether regional or national, reveals few nocturnes. Yet a night scene has a wealth of fascinating material for interpretation on canvas. Its avoidance by the amateur is understandable — right from the start it seems to be too difficult a subject to learn: just where or how does one begin?

Actually, however, a typical town or city nocturne can be simplified by treating it as you would the painting of a still life. Assuming that you do not have to contend with the elements of rain or snow, observation can be made and studies painted and continued on successive nights with few changes taking place. The artificial lights gleam regularly and the colored neon effects are the same night after night. Moving figures or objects will present some difficulties, of course, just as they would under any other lighting conditions. You must, to capture them on canvas, be keenly observant. Again, note how the artificial lights affect the local color of objects that you are familiar with in daylight. Observe how a red neon light bleaches out and heightens a red object and, in turn, makes green look black.

Studies made on a black or dark paper, with pastels used for color notes, provide an excellent basis for later canvases.

Canvases given a rub-in of a deep color or a dark stain are also helpful as a preparatory measure for subsequent painting. Details in the application of such a stain are given in the chapter on the use of the imprimatura.

Whenever possible, study the work of men who have painted nocturnes so well. John Sloan's "Election Night" and "Eve of Saint Francis," Pissaro's "Boulevard Des Italiens At Night," and Bellow's "Summer Night" are excellent examples.

The following demonstration is based on a sketch made with penciled color notations.

STEP 1. *Referring to the sketch above, a charcoal drawing is made. The distribution of the light and dark areas is also indicated in charcoal. The drawing is then sprayed with fixatif to hold the rough light and dark arrangement.*

STEP 2. *A limited color rub-in is given to the entire canvas, except for the light areas. This rub-in starts by using cobalt blue in all of the snow-covered areas. The same blue is then applied to the sky, and the cloud shapes are indicated with indian red. As the horizon is reached, a bit of yellow·ochre is added. While this toning of color proceeds, only the three colors mentioned are used. The green of the boats is suggested by the mixing of yellow ochre and cobalt blue. The extreme darks of the figures and other dark objects are arrived at by mixing the indian red and cobalt blue. A touch of black is added to these mixtures from time to time. This is done more to neutralize the over-all effect than to darken the colors.*

STEP 3. *Up to this stage the extreme light areas have still been held by allowing the white of the canvas to show through. These areas are now covered by a mixture of white paint with a slight touch of yellow ochre and cobalt blue. Even to this contrasting light mixture a wisp of black is added. From now to the completion of the subject the paint is gradually built up. Touches of cadmium red light are mixed with the indian red to brighten up the buildings and the train. Cadmium yellow light is used in the window and sparingly in the yellow ochre mixture of the wall in back of the house. The light side of the boat also is brightened up, with cadmium yellow added to the mixture.*

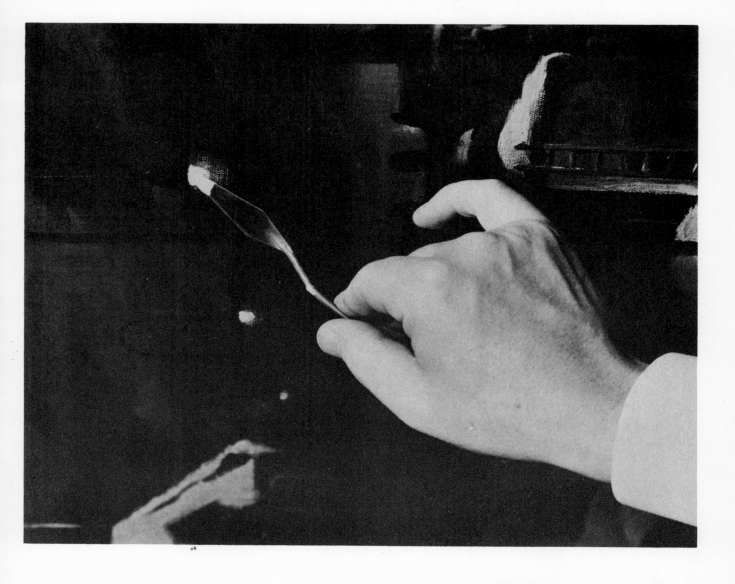

Below is shown how a dry-brush effect creates the glow of the electric light bulb. It is accomplished by dragging a flat bristle brush lightly over the rough canvas. No medium should be used and the canvas must be dry to achieve this effect.

The even more dazzling glow of the bulb itself is aided by applying the white paint heavily to the canvas with a painting knife as shown on the right. A touch of cadmium yellow light is added to the white to intensify its brilliance. This is the same principle as we used when suggesting glare over foliage, etc.

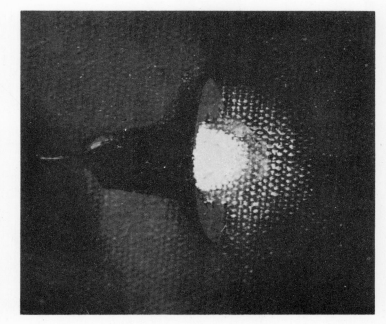

THE WINTER SUBJECT

Of all the seasons, I find winter to be the most interesting. The adverse weather conditions that often prevail are a stimulating challenge to the painter, particularly after a stint under the relaxing summer sun!

In reaching for subtle snow effects you will find, unless you are satisfied with "Christmas card" blue-violet shadows, that your powers of observation will be taxed to the utmost. To paint a snow scene with some degree of distinction, the obvious blues and purples must be toned down.

Many artists paint their winter subjects in the comfort of their studio by referring to pencil notes that have been made on the spot. However, this method is successful only after a long period of painting directly from nature.

Whenever possible, at the completion of a painting made outdoors, make one or two quick observation notes in color. Figures 1 and 2 are typical examples.

After doing a woodland sketch and before packing my painting equipment, I completed the day's work by making the color sketch shown in Figure 1.

The tree was not part of my original composition, but was made purely as a study complete in itself. The accompanying diagram gives an analysis of the color values.

Figure 2 is self-explanatory. The various formations of snow rooftops were painted on a 12-inch by 16-inch panel. This type of sketch is not primarily intended as a study but is material that can be incorporated into future studio paintings.

The extra time you spend in making such notes will result in the accumulation of data that will prove invaluable when you later paint indoors. The subject of our demonstration can be practiced by the hardy outdoor painter as well as by the studio painter — all one needs is a window with a fair view!

Although, when working indoors, you can proceed at a more leisurely pace than when working outdoors, the various stages of your painting should follow in the regular sequence. One advantage of working under such comfortable conditions is that you can carry the painting over to the following day if you wish. This is assuming that the lighting effect is approximately the same; generally, after a heavy snowfall only minor changes occur.

The contours of the terrain usually stay covered with a blanket of snow long enough to permit your working for at least two days. Probably the first definite change will be in the rooftops, as the heat from within the houses gradually melts the snow.

As your first day's work can be the accomplishment of the first three stages, you will have applied little solid paint to the canvas. Any minor changes or corrections can easily be made on the following day.

FIGURE 1

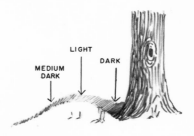

ANALYSIS OF CAST SHADOW

FIGURE 2

STEP 1. *The drawing is made directly on the canvas and the shaded areas indicated lightly with charcoal. It is then sprayed with fixatif.*

STEP 2. *The toning-in process is accomplished with french ultramarine. This color is ideal for the lay-in, as it is most harmonious with the winter subject.*

STEP 3. *The color application be-*
gins with the shaded areas. To
insure free handling, hold the
brush some distance from the
ferrule, rather than gripping it
as you would a pencil. Paint the
cast shadows of the snow as
closely as possible in the correct
color, using the white of the can-
vas to gauge the values. At this
stage the trees are still the french
ultramarine color of the original
lay-in.

STEP 4. *The trees are now*
painted, along with the leaves.
The light areas are then painted,
and the entire canvas is covered
except for the light snow and sky
areas. Still work in as free a man-
ner as possible. Any tightening
up or refining that is necessary
will be done at the final stage.

Paint the sky around and between the branches of the tree. The thinner branches and the leaves can be blurred easier and the twigs given a "lost and found" appearance. (See color plate on the following page.) The same principle applies to the distant hill — it appears more distant when the sky is painted to its edge. An atmospheric look is given to the painting by this procedure. This is particularly effective when the tree and distant hills are completely dry before the sky is painted.

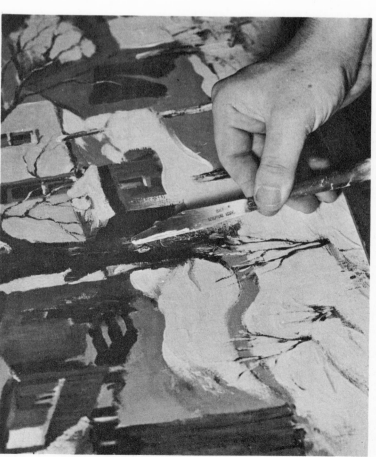

The light snow areas are painted heavily, adding to the feeling of the ground underneath being thickly blanketed. The photograph above shows a method of using the painting knife with a sparing amount of paint dragged across the base of the tree to impart a look of clinging snow. The tree should be dry when this is done. When applying such a stroke it is often much easier to accomplish it by reversing the position of the hand and knife as shown on the right. This enables you to control as well as see the effect as the stroke is executed.

CASEIN AS A BASE FOR OIL PAINTING

The use of casein paint as an underpainting for a subsequent oil painting is becoming increasingly popular.

While casein is a most versatile medium, here we will deal with it in relation to oil painting. Of primary importance is the surface upon which casein color is to be applied. You can use canvas if it possesses an absorbent surface. There are both cotton and linen canvases available that are especially prepared for the use of casein paint. While casein paint should never be applied heavily at any time, you must be particularly careful to work thinly when using a resilient surface such as canvas. The gesso panel makes an excellent base for underpainting. Besides being a rigid support it possesses a high degree of absorbency.

A 100% rag watercolor paper can be used as well as any tinted rag paper. Again, a rigid support should be arranged by first mounting the paper on a board or obtaining a commercially prepared watercolor board. You can use the same type of sable and bristle brushes that you use for oil painting. The sable brushes will probably be used most, as they facilitate the handling of flat underpainting. A filbert sable brush will be found to be excellent in the manipulation of casein. It is a cross between a long-haired, flat brush and a round brush, combining the best features of each. Brushes should always be washed with soap and water immediately after use because the casein becomes insoluble after a short period.

Casein paints come in a tube and in a wide range of colors. There is no need to re-orient your way of mixing color as the pigments are the same that are used in the making of your oil paints.

You need employ only water as a medium, but it is imperative that it be used every time the casein paint is applied. There is always a tendency for the novice to omit using water, for the casein paints often seem to possess a workable quality as they are squeezed from the tube. As a precautionary measure, always wet the brush before mixing any colors. There are several ways that casein can be used preparatory to the oil painting. You can plan a rough color scheme directly on the canvas or panel. Any changes you desire can then

Below is an example of the amount of detail and texture obtainable through the use of a casein base. By using a small sable pointed brush, you can render the most minute details. Casein, mixed in a light key, was used for the beach and water areas, with subsequent glazes of oil paint lowering the key and resulting in a rich, warm luminosity. This example has been reproduced about one-half the size of the original painting. It helps to convey in how detailed a manner you can work by using a casein underpainting. A gesso panel was used.

be made by washing out the area with a moist rag or sponge before repainting.

Once the color scheme is satisfactory, allow the surface to dry. This takes only a short while — a few hours being more than ample. Then cover the surface with a varnish to isolate it from the subsequent oil painting. While some artists use ordinary retouching varnish, there is a casein varnish made expressly for this purpose. A soft-haired brush should be used for applying the varnish. When you are finished, clean the brush with alcohol.

It is important to remember that only oil paints are to be used once the casein has been isolated. To attempt to use casein over varnish would risk the chance of it flaking off. What happens is that the varnished surface is no longer absorbent enough to act as a bond in holding the casein paint.

Besides using casein to develop the color scheme, you can employ it in rendering minute details. When you try to draw fine lines with oil paint, you find that you need quite a bit of turpentine or medium with which to cut the paint. Even then the lines are not crisp, but, instead, are inclined to be blurred. With casein, a pointed brush can be used and the finest line delineated. The area in which these details are needed can be retained in the finished oil painting. Once casein is varnished and oil

paint applied, it is visually impossible to tell the difference even though the later oil painting does not cover the entire casein underpainting.

There is a casein painting medium available that can be used to retard the drying of casein paint on any type of surface. Since casein dries very rapidly, this medium will prove most useful when covering large areas or when blending various tones of colors. This medium, which is a casein emulsion, is mixed with the water used to thin the paint.

In conclusion, mention should be made of the use of casein as a sketching medium. You will find it an excellent and convenient supplement to your oil equipment when on a sketching trip. You can make several color sketches or studies in casein as an aid in later studio painting. They are practically dry on completion and take up very little room. They can be placed on top of one another with no worry about them becoming smeared.

Although these casein sketches are done primarily as reference material, they often can be turned into attractive oil paintings. After having served their purpose as data, they can be subjected to the usual procedure of isolating the casein surface with varnish and then continued, until complete, with oil paint.

FROM CASEIN . . .

LEFT. *The subject is quickly rendered on the spot, using casein diluted to a watery consistency and painted on a watercolor board. A similar effect could be obtained on a gesso panel.*

. . . TO OIL

RIGHT. *Back in the studio the casein painting is covered with an isolating varnish (a special casein varnish). Oil glazes, followed by some of the areas vitalized with direct oil painting, resulted in this picture.*

Illustrated below is the use of casein as an underpainting for oil.

The first illustration shows the entire canvas covered with casein. Light, neutralized colors are used for the general over-all effect, for we are planning to use the oil glazes over these areas until the desired intensity of color is attained. At the same time details are rendered that will be retained as part of the finished painting.

After the casein base is thoroughly dry, give it an isolating coat of varnish. Incidentally, this coating will brighten the over-all effect, because the varnish changes the surface from mat to semigloss. You can start glazing with oil paint as soon as the surface is dry to the touch. If the varnish that isolates the casein is omitted, the subsequent oil glazes will gradually sink into the canvas, resulting in a dull, dead effect.

Use copal oil medium to cut the oil paint when glazing. The final color will result from a series of superimposed glazes that may be both warm and cool. From the start, the final result should be visualized and the glazes applied accordingly.

THE CASEIN UNDERPAINTING

COMPLETED WITH OIL GLAZES

STEP 1. *In this demonstration a gesso panel was used for the painting. Full details are given in the following chapter of the possibilities of the gesso base for painting directly with oils. The reason for using a panel for this demonstration is that a rigid surface is desirable if quite an amount of casein color is to be applied. However, canvas can be used so long as precautions are taken to apply the casein thinly — that is, using plenty of water.*

To take advantage of the fast-drying qualities of casein, a warm neutral grey color is brushed over the entire panel. This gives us a pleasant tone to work into and dries almost immediately after it has been applied. Using a pointed sable brush, the drawing is made in a burnt umber.

STEP 2. *As the nature of this subject is one that is made up of a series of definite strong forms, the casein color is applied in a precise manner, following these forms. An almost poster-like effect results as the picture starts to develop.*

STEP 3. *The casein painting continues with the light areas laid in. You will note how quickly a simple tonal arrangement of the dark middle-tone and light areas is arrived at. It is the over-all preparatory warm grey toning that aids in quickly establishing a middle-tone base.*

STEP 4. *Still applying the casein color in a poster-like fashion, care is exercised to allow the original grey middle-tone to remain in certain areas. By referring to the color plate, you can see that these areas include the shaded side of the white rocks, the shanty and its reflection, part of the water, and some of the portions of the large hill.*

STEP 5. *The casein underpainting is now complete. At this stage the over-all color pattern should be fairly flat. However, before applying any oil glazes or oil paint, you must first isolate the casein surface by covering it with a varnish. Placing the painting in a horizontal position and using a soft-haired flat brush, apply a coating of casein varnish. The varnish is transparent and dries almost immediately. A semi-gloss effect is imparted to the surface of the painting. You will note that the gloss is more apparent in those areas where you have applied the casein in a heavier manner. This should not be cause for concern as it will not affect the oil painting that follows when the varnish is thoroughly dry.*

STEP 6. *By comparing the two color plates on the opposite page, you will immediately note that the top casein underpainting is much cooler than the completed picture below. This has been done purposely, as much more luminosity is achieved when the warm oil glazes are applied over this cool undertone. Alternating glazes of raw sienna followed by cadmium yellow light are applied over the main areas of the painting. A warm blue glaze over the water and sky areas follows, care being taken that the clouds are not touched, as they are then covered with a delicate pink glaze. Some direct oil painting is resorted to in lightening the water in the middle area as well as the green in the large hill. The painting is completed with the details painted in a direct manner also.*

The detailed area reproduced below will give you some idea of the textural possibilities of this method of working.

The flat, over-all neutralized color pattern of the casein painting is shown above. Below is the result after oil glazing and direct painting have been accomplished. Note how the original grey tone has been held throughout the painting in the shadow side of the shanty and rock areas.

PAINTING ON A GESSO BASE

Gesso has been used as a painting ground for several centuries. It was popular during the Florentine Renaissance and has been universally accepted as the best permanent painting ground. While a gesso solution can be applied to canvas to increase its whiteness, it must be done in a thin manner, as it is susceptible to cracking on so flexible a surface. A panel, by providing a more rigid support, eliminates this hazard.

The following demonstration was painted on an already prepared gesso panel made of Presdwood. It is possible to make your own panels, but it is a time-consuming task. There are several commercial products available, and it is advisable to purchase one for your initial experiments. I use a panel identified as Durapan and have found it to be a most reliable base for painting both in oil and casein.

The gesso panel can be used just as it is for casein paints, but its very absorbent surface makes painting on it directly with oil more difficult. This absorbency can be reduced by applying a coating of a very thin shellac over the gesso surface preparatory to painting with oil. Casein varnish can also be used to cover the surface to make it more receptive to oil paint.

In this demonstration, a charcoal drawing was made directly on the original absorbent gesso ground. It was then sprayed with casein varnish (which contains a shellac base) thus fixing the drawing and reducing the surface absorbency in one operation.

The intense sparkling white of a gesso base imparts a great brilliance to the oil painting. Its smooth surface allows the painting of the most meticulous detail desired. The soft sable brushes can be used to advantage, but care must be taken to avoid excessive slickness.

The painting can be completed by glazing, the smooth finish of the gesso board forming a most sympathetic surface on which to manipulate glazes.

LEFT. *The sketch book is used to make a black and white wash brush drawing to establish the dark and light pattern. Casein black is used, diluted to a watery consistency for fast handling.*

BELOW. *When dry, a piece of tracing paper is placed over the drawing. Using a ball pen or a fairly hard pencil, a tracing is made and color notations indicated. Details of this method of making color notes are described on page 106.*

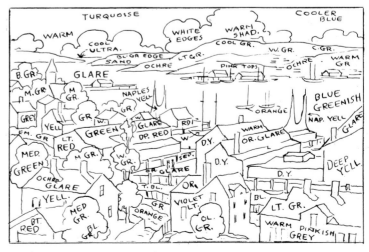

STEP 1. *Placing the sketches in a convenient position so they can be referred to easily, redraw the subject carefully. Use a charcoal pencil and keep it well sharpened throughout the drawing. When completed, a casein varnish is sprayed over the entire surface. This fixes the drawing and makes the gesso board less absorbent at the same time. If ordinary fixatif is used, a coat of thinned shellac should follow, unless you prefer working into an absorbent ground. In that case, omit the coating of shellac.*

STEP 2. *Whether covered with casein varnish or shellac, the gesso surface dries quickly. Starting with the immediate foreground, the approximate shadow colors are laid in. You will note that the hard surface of the gesso panel is not as receptive to your brush stroke as the more resilient canvas. Keep the paint thin, using medium to cut the paint and to facilitate handling. The flat sable brushes will be found excellent when painting on this type of surface as long as care is taken not to become over-slick.*

STEP 3. *The painting progresses by placing the approximate colors in the light areas. In this demonstration our approach is more deliberate as the color areas have already been planned in our preliminary sketch. What we are now doing is filling in carefully drawn areas with color, gradually covering the panel. You will find this method of working most helpful when doing an assignment that must be executed both rapidly and accurately.*

The use of the pointed knife is illustrated above. By careful manipulation small painted areas can be scraped and the original brilliant white gesso base will show through. In this painting the white masts, the rigging, and some of the minute highlights were indicated by this method.

STEP 4. *The water and distant hills are now painted. The sky area follows, allowing the white gesso panel to remain as the cloud shapes. The refining of color now begins and details are gradually added. The round bristle brush is used in a pouncing manner to give texture to the trees. A warm glaze is applied over the cloud areas and their shadow side is rendered in a subtle grey. The painting is completed by adding a warm glaze wherever the area appears to be too cool. (Details of glazing are given in a later chapter.)*

PALETTE KNIFE PAINTING

Earlier in this book, when the approach to painting was described, I stressed the drawing-in of the subject. I observed that the student often becomes confused if the drawn outline is lost too soon. Although the previous demonstrations have included the outline (drawing) and the monochromatic lay-in as separate stages, it is quite possible that eventually your work may become too tight unless the procedure is occasionally varied.

One excellent means of overcoming any tendency towards over-tightness is the use of the knife in the place of brushes. While a roughly sketched charcoal line drawing may be resorted to in order to indicate the main lines of the composition, the actual painting is done with the knife. It might be well to explain here the term "palette-knife painting," since it often confuses the student during the early stages of his study.

Palette-knife painting is the technique of applying color with a knife. The knife used is made of finely tempered steel and is far more flexible than the stiffer palette knife listed in art supply catalogues. The latter's chief functions are to remove left-over paint from the palette, to scrape off unwanted dried paint that may have accumulated on the canvas and, on occasion, to mix colors on the palette. The palette knife commonly used for these functions has a blade approximately four inches long. The more popular design is trowel shaped, as it is less awkward to handle when scooping up the paint (see below).

However, it is the knife for painting in which we are interested here. The two knives shown on either end of the group are the best for general all-around painting, with the other types to be gradually added to the collection as needed. As more work is done in this technique and its potentialities are explored, you may even wish to improvise knives to achieve additional textural effects.

Skies that have been painted in the accepted manner with the brush can often be made more interesting by using the knife to suggest clouds or light breaking through a clouded sky area. It is an excellent way to provide a strong highlight where the paint must be loaded on. By using the knife, you can brighten areas that have become dull from the continual brushing on of color. It is a method that gives an immediate appearance of strength and vitality to your subject.

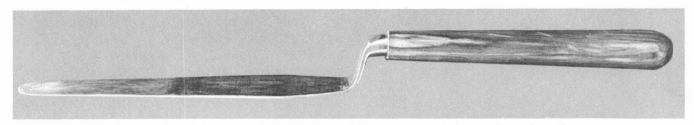

Above is shown the palette knife that is used for removing used paint from the palette, scraping of unwanted wet or dry paint from the canvas, or occasional mixing of colors in place of the brush. Below is pictured a selection of painting knives.

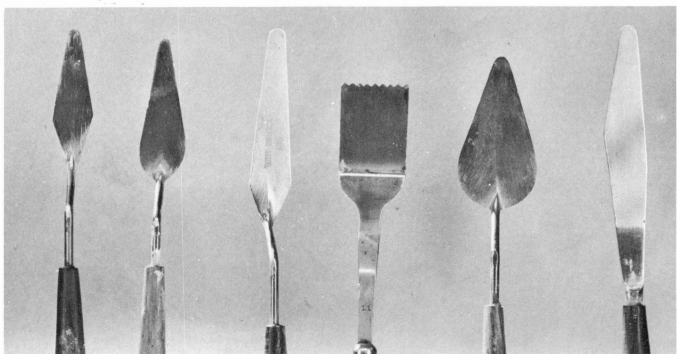

One way to bridge the gap from the drawing to direct painting with a knife is to use a color stain. After the drawing is completed and the surplus charcoal dusted off or sprayed with fixatif, a wash of colors thinned with turpentine can be applied with a brush or rag. This stain will guide you in determining the distribution of color that can be applied immediately with the knife.

The Drawing

The Stain

The Knife

In the demonstrations of subjects in this book I mention the painting knife whenever it can help you obtain certain results. Illustrated above are the three basic steps of painting, using only the knife.

The first step is the drawing, like that rendered when the brush is to be used. Then comes the toning in, using full color but applying it thinly and scraping it down whenever the paint accumulates too heavily.

In the final stage the entire canvas is covered with paint of varying thickness, typical of palette-knife painting. The close-up shows the initial application of paint, covering the dark areas first to determine the pattern.

On the following pages is a step-by-step demonstration of palette-knife painting. There is a tendency to use the brush occasionally to permit easier handling of a minute detail, but use only the knife for you should become familiar with its advantages as well as with its disadvantages. Characteristic of the technique is the ridge of paint that is left each time the loaded knife is pressed against the canvas. If the ridge is too heavy you can scrape it down with the edge of your knife. You will find that you will need more paint than when using a brush, so squeeze plenty of color on the palette when preparing to use the knife.

DEMONSTRATION OF PALETTE KNIFE PAINTING

STEP 1. *Make your drawing for a palette-knife painting in the same manner as in the previous demonstrations. Keep the charcoal sketch to a minimum of lines, as we want to do as much work with the knife as possible. Note how height is suggested by the mountain in the foreground by having its peak run out of the top of the canvas.*

STEP 2. *The dark side of the mountain is painted with the flat side of the knife. Mix as much of the color as possible directly on the canvas. The ridges of paint should be scraped down with the edge of the knife to prevent too early an accumulation of paint. You will soon discover that, compared to mixing with a brush, color mixed with a knife is fresher and much more vibrant.*

STEP 3. *The dark areas of the foreground and distant mountain are now painted. Do not attempt to hold the painting rigidly to the boundaries of the original outline. A major part of the charm of palette-knife painting is in its loose handling. At frequent intervals wipe the knife with a paint rag as you would the brush.*

STEP 4. *The closer mountain is now completely covered with paint. Vary the handling of the knife to aid you in modeling the form. Fan-like strokes with the edge of the knife start the shaping of the lighted area in the distant mountain. This step ends with the water in the foreground indicated and more color added to the strip of land in the lower right corner.*

STEP 5. *The painting continues until all of the canvas, including the sky, is covered. When doing the sky, keep your knife as flat as possible. This will be of aid in retaining an atmospheric quality. Later the cloud shapes can be modeled in short strokes with the tip of the knife, achieving a pleasing contrast to the sweeping flat strokes of the sky. The spotting of the local color of the houses is indicated, with no attempt made at this stage to design them into recognizable objects.*

STEP 6. *A check-up is made here and any heavy bits of rough paint that might be a disturbing note are scraped down. Generally you can allow the rough sections to remain in the foreground, to emphasize its nearness in contrast to the smoother background. The painting is completed with the adding of details to the house and foliage and a general over-all refining of the color.*

This close-up shows the palette knife that was used during the entire demonstration. Usually, when working on a large studio painting, I use several knives of various shapes. These facilitate the handling necessary to achieve a varied textural surface. As your interest in palette-knife painting grows, you will undoubtedly want to acquire more knives like those pictured on page 84.

One word of caution: If you are planning to do a palette-knife painting in several sittings, much more time must be allowed for drying periods as compared to painting with the brush. Paint put on a canvas with a knife piles up in heavy layers, taking much longer to dry thoroughly.

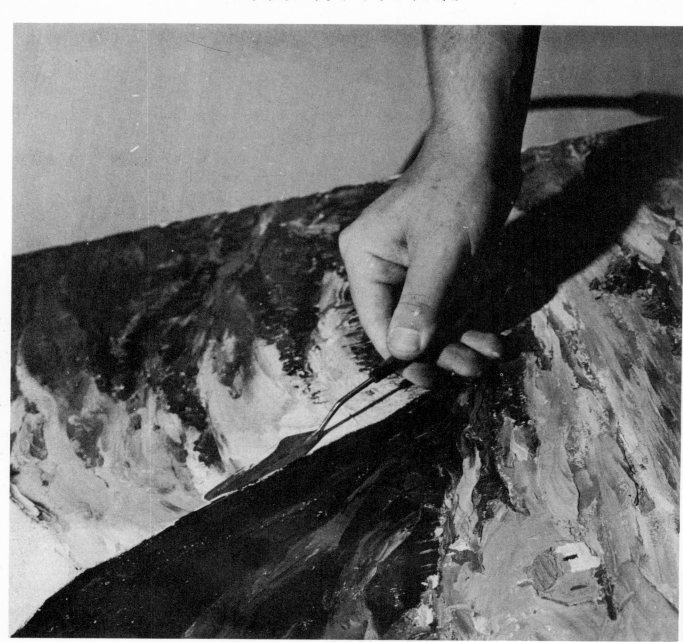

THE USE OF THE IMPRIMATURA

The imprimatura is a transparent glaze or stain that is laid over the canvas preparatory to the actual painting. This glaze or veil is applied to produce a sympathetic toning which eliminates the dull white of the canvas and at the same time affects the tonal quality of the painting. The transparent colors, such as burnt sienna, viridian, alizarin crimson, etc., are preferred, but opaque colors can be used if cut to a watery consistency.

Preparing an Imprimatura for Sketching. Copal varnish is poured into a saucer or paint pan. Squeeze a bit of color from the tube into the var-

nish and mix well. When it is thoroughly dissolved, dip a soft sable brush into the mixture and test its strength on the corner of the canvas. If it is the desired tone, proceed to cover the entire canvas with this stain. It does not have to be evenly laid, but the canvas should be in a horizontal position to prevent running of the stain.

The canvas is then put aside and allowed to dry, still in a horizontal position, until it becomes tacky. Then it can be leaned against the wall. When dry, make the drawing directly with a sable brush and follow with the painting, using your regular medium.

STEP 1. *In this demonstration the subject is first drawn in with charcoal. Dusting the surplus charcoal off the canvas until just a faint image remains, redraw the subject with india ink. This ink outline will remain visible as a guide throughout until heavy paint is applied.*

STEP 2. *Pour some copal varnish into a shallow saucer and squeeze in a bit of viridian. The viridian is mixed with the varnish until it is thoroughly dissolved. The varnish now resembles a green stain. Place the canvas in a flat or semi-horizontal position to control the flow of the stain. Dip a wide, flat sable brush into the mixture and start applying the stain at the top of the canvas and work downward. Keep working until the entire canvas is covered and do not be concerned about obtaining an evenly laid coat.*

92

How much the imprimatura affects the subsequent painting depends upon how thinly you work and how much of the stain can be retained in the final sketch. Some artists give their canvas panels an ocherish or greyish stain as an imprimatura when they are planning to work outdoors in the strong sun. With this foundation, any glare that might strike the panel is subdued and the strain on the eyes is greatly reduced.

Preparing the Drawing before the Imprimatura.
In doing a subject where more preliminary details may be desired, a charcoal drawing is made on the white canvas. Then it is sprayed with fixatif. Next,

the imprimatura is applied over the entire canvas either with the soft sable brush or a rag. The drawing will show through the transparent stain and act as a guide for the painting that follows.

There are several variations in the application of the imprimatura. A single color can be graduated in tone, being heavier at the base and lighter at the top (see chapter "Portrait of a House"). Or, again, other colors that have been reduced to a stain can be blended on the canvas.

You do not have to wait for the imprimatura to become thoroughly dry. If you are working directly from nature, you can begin the painting as soon as the stain becomes tacky.

STEP 3. *Right after the staining process, take a piece of lintless rag and wipe out the cloud shapes and the light area of the houses. Just as long as you have not allowed the stain to become tacky, the color can easily be removed. If by any chance you should have any difficulty, dip the rag into a small amount of turpentine to remove the stain.*

STEP 4. *The completed imprimatura is shown on the right. Note that the original ink outline still shows clearly through the color. Keep in mind that you are not necessarily limited to a single color stain. In your future work you may want to vary the application. The upper section of the canvas could be a cool color, blending into a warm tone at the base of the canvas.*

The reproduction above shows the painting at the conclusion of Step 5. Below is the finished result, with the trees, fences, rows of plants, and the rest of the details rendered. A figure is inserted to help direct the eye to the center of interest.

STEP 5. *Using our regular medium, the direct painting begins. Burnt sienna is the predominating color used on the sides of the houses, with alizarin crimson and french ultramarine mixed together for the rooftops where they appear a purplish color. The windows are left with the green stain showing through. The color reproduction on the left shows the painting at this stage.*

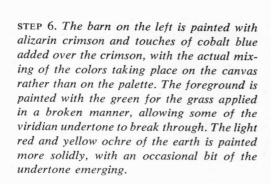

STEP 6. *The barn on the left is painted with alizarin crimson and touches of cobalt blue added over the crimson, with the actual mixing of the colors taking place on the canvas rather than on the palette. The foreground is painted with the green for the grass applied in a broken manner, allowing some of the viridian undertone to break through. The light red and yellow ochre of the earth is painted more solidly, with an occasional bit of the undertone emerging.*

STEP 7. *The painting continues with the distant hills rendered in cobalt blue. For an atmospheric effect, use a paint rag to remove some of the blue at the base. The green hills are then painted thinly, with quite a bit of the undertone showing through. Directly in back of the rooftops the undertone remains, creating a halo effect. This acts as an aid in recessing the hills and bringing the houses forward. Some yellow ochre is scumbled into the green hills to suggest fields. Start toning the sky, using cobalt blue and alizarin crimson diluted with plenty of medium. A transparent glaze results and is used to model the cloud forms. Whenever the color appears too heavy, rub it down with a rag so that the color will blend with the underpainting.*

GLAZING AND SCUMBLING

Glazing is used to enhance or modify previously painted areas. You can achieve greater transparency and depth of tone by glazing a light underpainting than you can by painting directly on the canvas. While the transparent colors of your palette (viridian, alizarin crimson, burnt sienna, etc.) lend themselves readily to this process, you can glaze with any color that has been sufficiently cut with medium.

There are prepared mediums obtainable for glazing purposes; the demonstration of one of them is shown in a later chapter. You can make your own glaze medium by mixing one part damar varnish, one part stand oil, and five parts turpentine. For fast drying, add a touch of cobalt drier.

There are several variations of glazing mediums where the varnish is increased to impart a tackier quality. The glazes can be mixed in saucers or paint tins. The color is squeezed from the tube into the medium and thoroughly mixed. Care should be taken that the glaze is not too thin, otherwise it will run down the canvas.

The painting reproduced below was first sketched in charcoal on the canvas and sprayed with fixatif. A fast-drying white was applied in the areas where a raised or heavy effect was desired in the final painting. The crumbling wall of the building on the right was applied in a broken manner with a painting knife and a stiff bristle brush, still using only the white paint. Where the snow was to appear heavy in the final painting, it was built up at this stage in the same manner. The painting was then put aside to dry. It is most important that the white be thoroughly dry before starting the painting in full color.

Courtesy of Dee Day

Use a soft sable brush, or even a rag, at times, to apply the glaze. Arrive at the desired color and luminosity of tone by a series of successive glazes.

Warm and cool glazes can be superimposed and areas neutralized by glazing complementary colors over one another.

If the glaze accidentally overlaps into an adjoining area, immediately wipe the glaze off that area with a dry rag. You can manipulate the glaze more easily by placing the canvas in a horizontal position.

Scumbling differs from glazing — it is the application of a lighter opaque or semi-opaque mixture applied over a darker base. In glazing we use transparent tones that intensify the color over the underpainting, while scumbling is used to lighten or unify darker areas. Done in a broken manner, scumbling will make for interesting textural effects. For this process, the surface of the canvas should always be dry.

You can use your oil paint as it comes from the tube and apply it with a brush. It can be wiped over with a rag, allowing as much color as you wish to remain. Use an oil medium to cut the paint if you want a semi-transparent result. A rough-surfaced canvas or underpainting is most suitable, as the scumble can be dragged over such a surface to produce interesting broken-color effects.

While a large portion of the original charcoal drawing was lost by the various areas being covered by the white underpainting, enough remained to act as a guide for the subsequent painting. The canvas was then covered with thinned paint in the approximate color values. The painted passages were frequently wiped with a rag, allowing the color that remained to fill in the crevices of the white underpainting. The final effect was achieved through the combination of glazes of transparent colors and the scumbling of the more opaque colors. The detail shown below illustrates the textural quality obtained through this method.

UNDERPAINTING

Both the monochromatic lay-in, which preceded the painting in many of the demonstrations, and the imprimatura are forms of underpainting. We are now dealing with underpainting that influences the color as well as the texture of the final painting.

Underpainting should be planned and applied with the final color effect in mind. Since all of the steps are executed in the studio, it is helpful to have, as a guide, a color rough of the intended final picture in view during the entire painting. Use fast-drying colors with heavy body and little oil, and substitute flake white for the slower-drying zinc white. Transparent or staining colors should be avoided, along with the slow-drying paints.

As mat and as dull a surface effect as possible is desirable for an underpainting, for any paint that dries with a gloss is difficult to paint over. Colors can be used to act as a contrast or neutralizer for the final effect. For example, the sky can be painted a warm pink in the underpainting, and a cool blue painted or glazed over it in the final painting.

The underpainting should, in general, be kept in fairly light neutral colors. Avoid sharp accents of lights and darks. On the other hand, a dark area that you later intend to cover with a scumble or lighter broken colors in the overpainting, can often result in an interesting textural effect. A thoroughly dried surface is necessary before any overpainting is done. A small amount of cobalt drier will accelerate drying.

I previously mentioned the substitution of flake white or white lead for your regular white. There are white paints on the market that are especially made for underpainting. They set within a short period of time, drying any color that is mixed with them. The drying period can be retarded, if necessary, by simply adding the regular titanium or zinc white to the underpainting white.

STEP 1. *The order of preparing the underpainting is as follows: (1) The sky and the water beyond the bridge are painted in a warm pinkish tone. (2) A warm light ocherish tone is used for the foreground, middle, and distant land. (3) The trees, foliage, and distant hills are painted in various shades of pale green, with a touch of crimson as they come forward. (4) A pale blue with a touch of pink is used for the water in the immediate foreground. (5) The shaded areas of the rocks and houses are painted a warm earth red. (6) The glare effect on the road, rooftops, and rocks is suggested by applying white paint with a touch of yellow ochre in a heavy manner.*

STEP 2. *The painting is allowed to dry thoroughly. (1) Warm yellow and pink glazes are applied in an alternating fashion over the rock formations and houses. (2) The trees and foliage are covered with warm yellowish glazes. (3) A glaze of manganese blue in varying intensity is applied over the water areas, deeper in the foreground and lighter in the distance. (4) This stage is concluded with the same blue glazed over the sky.*

STEP 3. *The painting is now given an over-all checkup to determine the need for additional glazing. (1) Another glaze of manganese blue is applied over the water in the foreground, intensifying and enriching the color. (2) The color of the rocks is strengthened with additional alternating warm and cool glazes. (3) The blue of the water just beyond the bridge is intensified with another glaze; this acts to heighten the effect of the glare on the road and rooftops. (4) Some touches of cerulean blue are scumbled over the warm tones of the rocks; this should be done in a broken manner over a dry surface to achieve the texture of rock. (5) From now to the finish, details are gradually added, such as accents of dark in the rock areas to indicate crevices, and the modelling of trees and shrubbery. The chimneys with their long cast shadows that help emphasize the light are painted. The subject is completed with the painting of the sea gulls.*

GLAZING OVER A DRAWING

In the "Glazing and Scumbling" chapter a formula was given for reducing the oil paint to a transparent consistency.

There are already-prepared mediums on the market that are conveniently tubed. A small amount can be squeezed onto your palette and mixed with the oil paint to make the latter as transparent as desired. Its jelly-like quality reduces the most opaque of oil colors, and no additional medium of turpentine, oil, or varnish is needed to make it workable.

The following demonstration illustrates a method of holding the original drawing from the start to the finished stage. This method is of particular advantage when doing architectural subjects or whenever a tight or exact rendering is desired. It will also be found useful in experimenting with figure studies.

A figure drawing can be made in raw umber or oxide of chromium. When dry, the flesh tones can be mixed and cut with the glazing medium to a transparent consistency. Then the various flesh tones can be added with a soft sable brush. Now you are free to concentrate on the color because the drawing has already been established by the undertone of raw umber or oxide of chromium.

In this demonstration a glazing medium known as "Gel" was used. When this procedure is used, the finished result will resemble a colored drawing rather than an oil painting. The surface quality is naturally thin, as the color has been achieved with staining glazes instead of with the uncut, heavier oil paint.

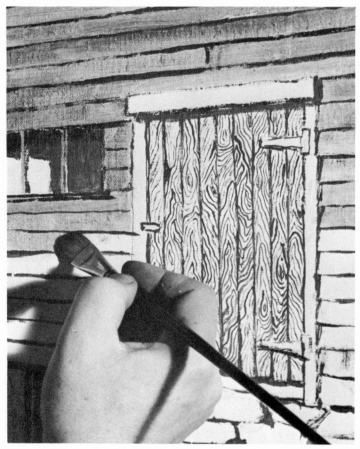

UPPER LEFT. *A drawing is made using raw umber mixed with enough fast drying medium to make it workable.*

ABOVE. *When the canvas is dry to the touch of your fingers, the glazing process can be started. Instead of using your regular medium, a small amount of the glazing medium described above is squeezed on the palette. A bit of it is mixed with your oil paints just before applying the color to the canvas. The color immediately becomes more transparent, yet it retains all of its original body characteristics. A soft sable brush is recommended here.*

LOWER LEFT. *The glazing processes are concluded and the painting is completed with a few crisp strokes of opaque paint.*

DEMONSTRATION OF
GLAZING AND SCUMBLING

STEP 1. *The subject is sketched in directly, using raw umber.*

STEP 2. *An underpainting is now prepared, using a fast-drying white. This should be flake white or an especially prepared underpainting white now on the market. As this white is mixed with the other colors, it will be of aid in accelerating their drying time. Our painting begins by giving the buildings, wall, and sidewalk a heavy coating of the fast-drying white. It is applied with a painting knife to suggest the broken wall surface. The color reproduction on the upper right of page 102 shows the distribution of the colors used for the underpainting. They are indian red, naples yellow, oxide of chromium opaque, cobalt blue, and burnt umber. These colors are applied both with the knife and with the brush to vary the texture.*

STEP 3. *At the conclusion of the previous step the underpainting is complete and is put aside to dry thoroughly. We are now ready to start the glazing process. A warm glaze of cadmium yellow light is applied over the entire area of the main house and stone wall. This is followed by a glaze of viridian over the shutters and door of the house. At the same time the viridian glaze is painted over the lawn between the houses. The step is concluded by toning the sky with a glaze mixed with cobalt blue and viridian, allowing some of the original warm pink undertone to remain as cloud shapes.*

101

STEP 4. *While waiting for the first of the series of glazes to dry, we can start working on the dark areas that are to be scumbled with lighter color. A mixture of light red, yellow ochre, and a touch of cobalt blue is scumbled over the brick area that breaks through the front of the house. A small amount of your painting medium can be used to cut this mixture if it is too heavy. Using a stiff bristle brush and a rag to wipe off any excessive accumulation of paint, the strong red brick area is subdued. However, bits of the original color are allowed to remain as shadows cast by the outer facing stone and as accents. A cool tone of cobalt blue, with touches of light red and oxide of chromium, is scumbled over the road. This same mixture, applied in a more broken manner, is then applied to the shaded areas of the second house. A warm violet is scumbled over the distant hill and is followed by spotting yellow and light green over the deep green hill. This area is shown in detail on the left.*

With the scumbling completed, the previously glazed areas are now checked to make certain that they are dry. A glaze of raw sienna is applied over the previous yellow glaze of the main house. Note how the raw sienna is made more brilliant by the underglaze of yellow. Cadmium orange is glazed over the rooftop of the second house, imparting a warm glow to the area. Glazes of cadmium yellow are applied over the lawn and the shutters of the house. From now to the finish the remaining areas are painted directly. The trees are reshaped, the cyclist repainted, and accents put in the crumbly walls with touches of burnt sienna.

The close-up reveals the scumbling effect that aids in giving texture to the wall of the house.

102

How the underpainting appears at the end of Step 2 is shown above. Below is the painting, complete with glazing and scumbling.

STUDIO PAINTING

Working methods from field notes

To the landscape painter, the time spent painting or sketching on the spot is invaluable, even indispensable. Certainly the scene must be witnessed first hand, for inspiration and details are obtained only from prolonged study directly from nature. While in time the artist may do all his larger and seemingly more important canvases in the studio, he constantly returns to nature, seeking new color schemes, forms, subject matter, and, most important, renewed emotional response.

Many factors decide at what time in his career the artist turns to doing what he considers his more ambitious, or at least more ambitiously planned, painting in the studio. Certainly subject matter is an important factor. A painter of metropolitan street scenes, for instance, after accumulating

THE SPOT PAINTING

enough on-the-spot sketches and studies, will find it much easier to concentrate on the painting of a large canvas by working indoors. Any fleeting effect in nature that may have been captured in a sketch has to be developed in the studio. Difficult on-the-spot working conditions on account of heat or cold may prevent completion of the painting, as will the rendering of constantly moving objects. The artist alone can determine whether it is feasible for him to return day after day to complete his painting when nature causes only minor changes in the scene. However, it is only after a long period of outdoor study that a reasonably convincing landscape in oil can be made in the studio; indeed, it has become possible for some painters (who have acquired this outdoor background) to do an oil painting in the studio that has all the conviction of having been done on the spot.

Certainly, in the quiet of his studio the artist can concentrate on strengthening the design, simplifying the masses, and developing the color scheme. And it is in the studio, too, of course, that the artist will prepare his undertones for later painting and will do the last refining.

However, it is his spot sketches that must supply the reference material for these studio paintings. In short, nature provides the inspiration for the original sketch.

Below and in the following two pages I describe various methods of working in the studio from field notes.

Whenever possible, the best method of accumulating data for subsequent studio work is the painting of the subject on the spot. Observing nature's colors and transferring them directly to the canvas is of paramount importance. Later in the studio the final composition can be developed and the drawing corrected.

THE STUDIO PAINTING

On the spot drawing with color notations

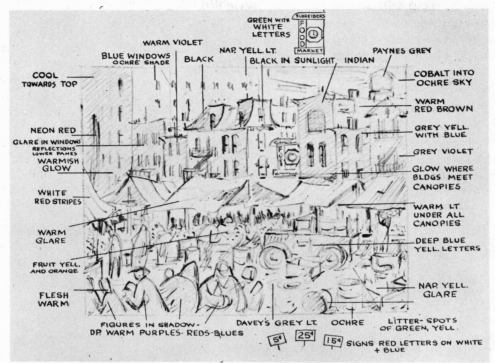

THE SPOT PAINTING

The black and white sketch, along with penciled notations, is of aid when it is not possible or feasible to paint the subject on the spot. It can be interpreted to best advantage only after you have acquired a background of painting directly from nature. The black and white sketch can also be used to supplement a painted sketch.

THE STUDIO PAINTING

The drawing and overlay combination

Another method of utilizing sketches and studies is through the use of the overlay.

A drawing can be made and fully rendered in light and shade directly from nature. When it is completed, lay a piece of tracing paper over the drawing. Then, using a pencil or fountain pen, make color notations.

This method allows you to make as elaborate a drawing as you wish. At the same time, you have the color notations plus the intact drawing.

All that is required is a tracing pad and some sheets of drawing paper cut to the same size. The drawing is made on the paper and then placed under the top sheet of the tracing pad. Notations are made

of the various colors on the tracing paper instead of on the drawing. A ball point fountain pen is excellent for indicating the notes as it is not as likely to indent the surface of the drawing underneath. In the illustrations shown below, the overlay also contains the traced outline of the subject. This can be omitted if time is limited, and just the notations made. The overlay and the drawing can always be keyed together later in the studio when they are needed as reference.

There are pads available that have a thin sheet of transparent paper between each leaf of drawing paper. While they were originally designed to protect the finished drawings, the pads can be converted to notation use.

The fragmentary sketch

Earlier in the book I mentioned how the most fragmentary of sketches are of far more value to the painter than the most detailed photograph.

However, before you are able to use a fragmentary sketch as a basis for a studio subject, you must first serve a long apprenticeship of painting directly from nature and you must store up a considerable amount of knowledge for future reference.

This method of working from a fragmentary sketch has advantages in that it forces the painter

to use his imagination and to invent color schemes, suggests necessary details, and helps him to capture all the subtleties of nature right in his studio. Thus, all of his resourcefulness and creative ability are brought into play.

THE STUDIO PAINTING
COURTESY OF WASHINGTON STATE COLLEGE

THE SPOT SKETCH

THE MAKING OF STUDIES

We have previously discussed various methods of sketching as a means of collecting material for future studio paintings. Along with the doing of sketches that are spontaneous interpretations of the scene before you, individual studies are required for details.

A sketch can be considered complete in itself, while a study is a detail that can be incorporated into the studio painting. Reproduced below is a group of such studies. They are typical of material that is very useful to refer to when planning and working on the studio painting. Actually these studies serve as supplementary data to sketches, which in turn supply the inspiration for the contemplated painting. In contrast to the sketch that often must be done swiftly to capture a passing effect, a study is a probing search for fact and form, a recording of what takes place in nature to the most minute detail.

These studies are not to be confined to painting alone but should also be rendered in black and white, using pencil as well as charcoal. The pencil with its fine point is invaluable in depicting the sharpest of details. Charcoal, a most fluent medium, has the advantage of quickly covering the broad masses of a subject as well as rendering details.

ACHIEVING A MORE DYNAMIC COMPOSITION

After a thorough period of painting on the spot, you arrive at a stage where you can produce a creditable representation on canvas. In all probability it is an honest, if literal, depiction of the subject, its artistic result depending on the amount of feeling that you have been able to transmit in your interpretation. It is quite possible that you have become quite a proficient painter, able to turn out an acceptable, if not an exciting, painting. To progress beyond this point, it is necessary that you seek out just what makes one interpretation ordinary, another exciting and more dynamic. One solution is to forego the usual painting of the subject on the spot and spend some time in the studio, there viewing past efforts and attempting to analyze just what is lacking.

Figure 1 is a painting made on-the-spot. All the elements are represented as they appeared with but slight changes from nature.

Figure 2 is a studio painting of the same subject, with the composition dramatized through re-arrangement of the masses of dark and light. The first important step was the changing of the

proportion of the canvas. By fitting the composition into a squarer proportion, I automatically had to place the lines at an angle more acute than the placid lines of Figure 1. The tonal masses were then rearranged, even to the extent of changing the contours of the hills and reversing the angle of the mountains. A close-up portion of a telegraph pole was inserted in the immediate foreground to add more depth to the receding poles.

I emphasized the forms by placing light edges alongside of dark areas, thus forcing the contrast. However, I had to take care not to make this "forcing" too obvious.

Additional textural quality was attained through the use of the palette-knife technique which helped to convey the rugged atmosphere of the subject. The houses were simplified so that they became part of the landscape rather than individual homes.

In short, in the studio painting I eliminated everything that seemed superfluous in the on-the-spot painting and emphasized any form that added impact to the painting's character or mood.

THE SPOT PAINTING

THE STUDIO PAINTING

DEMONSTRATION OF CHANGING PROPORTION

The pencil drawing reproduced above, from my sketch book, was made on the spot. It became the basis of a studio painting in which I made the following changes to add interest and impact. I changed the composition lines automatically by redrawing the subject on a canvas of a squarer proportion. As many placid, even, horizontal lines as possible were eliminated, with emphasis placed on any wavering lines such as those of the dock and boathouse rooftop. I left enough of the house on the right in the composition to form a vertical bulwark and to keep the horizontal lines from running out of the picture.

At the same time, more foreground was added to form a more substantial base.

To convey the impression of the height of the hill in the background, the lines of its contours were raised. I further strengthened this impression by showing less sky and allowing some of the trees to break beyond the top line of the composition. A figure was placed in the act of working at the side of the boat, to add a touch of activity to the scene. When the toning of the canvas began, as much as possible of the composition was painted in big masses. Light and dark areas were placed side by side for emphasis and rearranged wherever I felt it helped the composition. The massing of the house on the right side, along with the foreground, is an example.

In the final painting, shown at the bottom, all the details that I thought necessary were put in. The painting was concluded with a gradual over-all refining of color and simplifying of areas.

In summation, I believe that it is better to achieve as much impact, through over-emphasis if necessary, at the stage when the composition is redrawn on the canvas. Then, as you paint, any areas or objects that seem distorted can be modified. It should be kept in mind that many areas or shapes that seem to be only mildly emphasized in line can appear to be overdone when color is applied.

INTRODUCING FIGURES INTO A LANDSCAPE

The spotting of a figure in the appropriate place in a landscape is most important. While it may not be necessary to be an accomplished figure painter to insert one or several incidental figures into a composition, they should be convincingly indicated.

Quite frequently you can heighten the dramatic effect of a painting by the skillful placing of figures. A landscape which contains a road or houses of any prominence whatsoever looks most desolate when lacking the human element, and it is well-nigh impossible to omit figures in a street scene!

As a source of subject material, study figures while you sketch from nature. Figure 1 is a typical example of what can happen when sketching. While I was doing a pencil drawing in a small Pennsylvania town, the street was deserted except for the cars pulled to the side of the road. Suddenly a figure emerged from around the bend, walking toward me. I hurriedly spotted it in with little more result than a smudge on the sidewalk. Anxious to obtain more detail, I made a quick sketch in the only available blank space left on the drawing — the unfinished sky area.

Later, in my studio, when I developed a painting from the sketch, the figure that was so in character with the surroundings made an excellent authoritative note.

FIGURE 1

Make sketches whenever possible of people at work, at play, standing and sitting alone or in groups, walking, lolling on the beach, etc. The accumulation of such sketches will serve a double purpose: an improvement in drawing and a source of reference material when you need figures for a painting.

Keep the drawing simple. Just show the main lines of action when the figure is in motion. When the figure is in repose, give more consideration to the silhouette.

FIGURES IN A LANDSCAPE

At the bottom of this page is a reproduction of my painting, "Carolina Maneuvers."

The painting was developed from rough notes and sketches, some of which are reproduced here. I had to depend upon memory for most of the color, as my penciled notations were vague. The landscape was simple to paint — I had merely to depict cor-

rectly the distinctive features of the rolling hills — but the figures were a problem. All their movements were synchronized, and at a given time each man was performing a specified maneuver. Instead of worrying about getting details drawn in, I concentrated on spotting the figures in as correct a position as possible. I could take care of the details later!

DEMONSTRATION OF COMPOSING MOVING FIGURES IN A LANDSCAPE

This demonstration differs from the previous ones because either the circumstances under which the subject is to be painted are not favorable for any prolonged or there is not enough time available for the preliminary construction.

In this subject the moving figures, the fast changing light, and the cold weather all contribute to make working conditions difficult. To paint a color sketch as soon as possible, however rough, is highly desirable. The plan in this demonstration is to execute the finished painting in the studio. It is important that you also take time, before or after the painting of the color sketch, to make some penciled notes of the moving skaters for reference (see Figure 1). Refer to the notes whenever figures are to be spotted in during the studio composition. To do without these drawing notes, depending instead on painting them directly on the spot, requires far greater experience than the average student possesses.

At the same time, a drawing of the entire scene is made on paper to serve not only as a preliminary composition, but to be referred to also for additional data while doing the studio painting. Shown below are the drawing and the painted sketch that are to serve as the setting for the skaters. When doing the latter, paint the colors which dominate the scene immediately after the construction lines are roughly indicated. Use a generous amount of medium to facilitate the application of paint. Details are eliminated, as we are concerned only with the general over-all effect.

If you feel that you are capable of putting in some of the moving skaters at this time, by all means do so. Paint as fast as possible, making every attempt to capture the spirit of what is taking place before you.

Do not try to delineate the figures carefully. Later when the final painting is composed in the studio, they can be drawn carefully by referring to the preliminary pencil sketches. Our primary concern when painting on the spot is the acquisition of authoritative color notes.

FIGURE 1

THE SPOT DRAWING

THE SPOT PAINTING

STEP 1. *With your notes before you and the general composition in mind, the construction lines are quickly roughed in. As we are trying to capture the spirit of the subject when first observed, it is best not to be restricted to too exact a drawing.*

STEP 2. *The painting is started by working directly in color. Work in as flat a manner as possible at this stage, imagining that you are painting on the spot. As the foreground, trees, and background take shape, as in a stage setting, the actors (the skaters in our case) are placed in position. At the conclusion of this step the rough over-all color effect should convey the feeling that the painting was done outdoors.*

STEP 3. *This is the most difficult stage, because in modeling the various forms and pulling the painting together the spirit of the subject can often be lost. The use of the painting knife whenever possible will help to retain the vitality of the subject.*

All of us arrive at a period when we go a bit stale. It often comes at a time when we feel we have reached a saturation point in the doing of a certain subject matter. It may not be convenient to seek new material, but the feeling is strong to paint something different!

That is the time I find it profitable to browse through notebook sketches for new subject matter. The paintings at the bottom of each of these pages provide examples of the eventual use of material from such sketches.

Looking through a notebook devoted to a series of backyards and side-street drawings, I saw one that seemed to lend itself to further development (see upper left).

Continuing to go through more sketch books, from three different sources I found material that possessed definite possibilities for use in a painting that was developing in my mind's eye. They included some sketches I had made in a school playground of some children dancing, a group of men playing cards on a Gloucester dock, and some park sketches of mothers sunning their children. A drawing of an automobile of ancient vintage completed the necessary notes.

All of the sketches were of poses that were in keeping with the spirit of the subject I wished to paint. After some preliminary planning, the sketches were transposed into a comprehensive charcoal drawing before I did the final painting.

THE SOURCE MATERIAL

THE STUDIO PAINTING

MATERIAL FOR STUDIO PAINTINGS

The procedure in the accumulation of material for the painting at the bottom of this page was similar to that for the previously described subject.

The task in this case was less arduous because all of the source material needed was found in one notebook. Along with sketches, I had made several studies of an excavation subject. All of these were incorporated into a carefully rendered charcoal composition directly on the canvas and then sprayed with fixatif. A rough color lay-in was then indicated thinly on the canvas. The color scheme itself was invented, as I had made only a few notations on my sketches of the actual colors. The finished painting finally evolved by the gradual addition of heavier layers of paint to the original lay-in of thin color.

THE CHARCOAL COMPOSITION

THE ROUGH COLOR LAY-IN

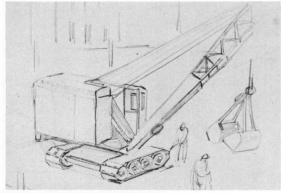

THE SOURCE MATERIAL

THE FINISHED PAINTING

USING A SHEET OF GLASS AS AN AID

IN COMPOSING VARIOUS ELEMENTS

In an earlier chapter I mentioned the spotting of figures on a sheet of glass preparatory to placing them on canvas.

On the right is a tonal lay-in of a studio painting. It has been carried to a stage where all of the elements that make up the composition have been indicated, with the exception of the seagulls. As the gulls form a vital part of the picture, it is important to place them in the most pleasing arrangement.

Below is shown the painting of the gulls on a sheet of glass that has been placed over the canvas. The glass can then be moved around the canvas until the gulls assume a satisfactory position in relation to the rest of the composition.

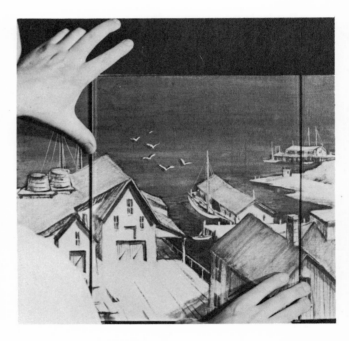

In trying to find the most advantageous position on the canvas, I felt that more gulls were needed, so I proceeded to add to the formation on the glass. Later, on checking the formation, I did not hesitate to remove any of the gulls that I found did not aid the composition. I removed them by simply rubbing them off with a rag slightly moistened with turpentine.

Finally, having arrived at what I thought to be the best arrangement, I carefully noted the composition, removed the glass, and proceeded to paint the gulls directly on the canvas. The finished painting is shown at the left.

DRAMATIZING A SUBJECT

Several years ago in Provincetown, I painted a typical beach scene of men working around the boats with a nearby wharf forming the background.

It was a serene day and the subject matter, although picturesque, was not particularly exciting. The painting was just another sketch to add to the collection of my summer's work.

A few years later I read about a hurricane striking Provincetown; it was severe enough to cause considerable damage. In my studio, hundreds of miles away from the scene, I attempted to visualize in my mind's eye what was taking place. Immediately I thought of using the storm as a subject for a painting, and I thumbed through an accumulation of Cape Cod sketches that might serve as a back-

ground. Discarding several possibilities, I finally decided upon the sketch described above — its very quiet, sunny quality offering a challenging contrast to the mood I had in mind to paint.

On a 30-inch by 40-inch canvas and with the sketch before me, I proceeded to compose the picture, using a piece of soft charcoal to indicate the large masses.

The quiet mood of the sketch was aided by a long, horizontally proportioned canvas, and horizontal lines dominated the composition; but the studio canvas was rectangular in shape, so I redesigned the lines at a more acute angle. I shortened horizontal lines, retaining only those that acted as a foil, to emphasize the movement of the angular lines.

Not only were the cloud shapes changed and the sky tone lowered, but trees were improvised in the background to help convey the feeling of the blowing gale. Even incidental objects, like the small rowboat that was only partially indicated in the sketch, became tossing objects, and the wash straining at the clothes line contributed to the over-all dramatic effect.

THE SPOT PAINTING

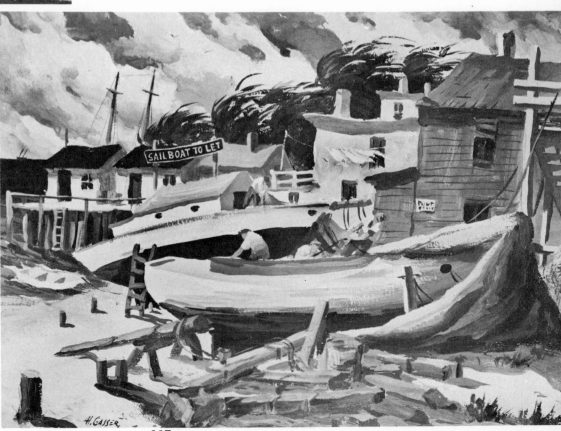

THE STUDIO PAINTING

DEMONSTRATION OF DRAMATIZING A SUBJECT

A subject similar to that on the preceding page has been chosen for this demonstration of the dramatizing of a sketch.

The painting reproduced below is of a typical dock scene painted on a summer day. Except for the activity of the few men at work, the subject is a quiet one with a maximum of horizontal lines. The serene sky adds an over-all peaceful effect.

Using this scene as a basis for the demonstration, we shall proceed to recompose the subject in order to increase the dramatic aspect and make it as exciting as possible.

To do this we shall assume that a sudden storm is approaching. Every possible device is employed to help convey this impression. The men who have hitherto been working around the boat most casually are now galvanized into action. They are redrawn into figures straining and pulling in their effort to make everything as secure as possible before the storm breaks. Whenever possible, straight horizontal and vertical lines are placed at a more acute angle.

On the next page is a step by step text description of the painting procedure I used to achieve the final painting.

STEP 1

STEP 2

THE SPOT
PAINTING

STEP 1. *Destroy the serenity of the spot painting by accenting as many diagonal lines as possible and minimizing horizontal lines. The swirling cloud shape is a typical example as are such devices as emphasizing the action of the various figures, the overturned can, and objects blowing in the wind.*

STEP 2. *While in Step 1 we depended upon line alone to convey the effect we are trying to capture, we are now aided by tonal values. The cloud shape is accented by rubbing in a dark blue tone behind it. This same lowering of the sky tone emphasizes the light masts of the boats tossing about. At the conclusion of the rubbing in of the blue tone, we have arrived at a fairly good conception of the effect of the redistributed values.*

STEP 3. *Color now makes its contribution to our subject. Starting with the dark areas, paint the color thinly, rubbing it into the canvas where it meets the light areas. Use a limited number of colors, mostly of the earth variety, and thus impart a low over-all key. A very slight touch of black added to the rest of the colors as they are applied to the canvas will aid in controlling the low key.*

STEP 3

STEP 4. *As the canvas is gradually covered with paint, care must be exercised when the light areas are painted. Since we have been using a low key, the light areas are likely to jump forward too much. By the same token, any bright spot of color will sing out strongly, so make certain that it is placed in a position which will aid the composition. It is in the subtle transposition of values and color that we really attain a more dramatic quality, rather than in the obvious darkening of the threatening sky.*

STEP 4

THE PAINTING

DRAMATIZED

PAINTING A PORTRAIT OF A HOUSE

Possibly the closest many landscape painters ever come to doing a portrait is when they are called upon to do a historic building, monument, or even a house.

Before I ever received such an assignment, I thought nothing of eliminating several windows, moving chimneys to one side, changing the local color, or even reducing a two-story house to one story! Just as long as it fitted better into my composition, I felt justified in taking such artistic liberties.

When confronted by a well known historic building with 50 windows visible, painting becomes more of a problem. It is true that an architectural rendering is not needed or desirable, but no matter how vaguely suggested, 50 windows have to appear. There is always someone who will count them!

Taking pains to study the subject at different times of the day under various lighting conditions will often help to minimize unpleasant or ornate details. Rearrangement of shadows and skillful improvising of cast shadows will also prove helpful, particularly in overcoming the problem of many windows. Doing a house, especially if the surrounding terrain is colorful, is less difficult. Unlike the historic subject, which usually must be approached from a limited angle so that it is quickly recognized, the house can often be painted from several positions. (I am assuming that the owner is right when he says that his house has good lines and is attractive from any angle!)

In the demonstration that follows, the house was designed so that the front faced the high rolling hills. After circling around the house, I felt that the best arrangement to paint was the view from the back. From this angle I could include the rolling hills. As it was autumn, they formed a beautiful colored background against the black rooftops of the house. I began by making a quick casein color sketch, but spent most of my time making pencil studies with notations. Two of these are reproduced below. The first shows the entire composition that I planned to use when painting the subject in the studio. In the second note, still within the same angle of view, I moved closer to the house, as there were some details that I wanted to record.

On returning to my studio, I placed the various pencil drawings and the color sketch before me. Taking a fairly smooth white canvas, I proceeded to sketch the composition, using charcoal, and referred to the note below.

Details of how the painting was developed are given in the following step-by-step demonstration.

STEP 1. *As the subject is to be painted against an autumn background, a warm stain over most of the canvas will help to achieve a harmonious effect and a pleasing surface to work on. After the composition is sketched on the canvas with charcoal, dust it lightly, allowing a faint image to remain. Then, using a small, pointed sable brush, carefully make a detailed drawing, using a waterproof ink. While the ink is drying pour some copal varnish into a saucer and squeeze a bit of burnt sienna into it. Mix it well. Then, using a soft sable brush or rag, cover the entire canvas. (In this particular case I gradually lightened the stain as it neared the top of the canvas so as not to give the sky area too strong an undertone. What we are doing is applying an imprimatura to the canvas. See the chapter, "The Use of the Imprimatura.")*

STEP 2. *As soon as the imprimatura becomes tacky, generally in a very short time, start the painting. The roof of the house, being black, is painted first, followed by the white areas of the house. You will note how an immediate range of values is established — the darkest being the roof, the burnt sienna stain forming a middle-tone, and the white area of the house the lightest value. The painting proceeds with the spotting of the various colors that are adjacent to the house. As soon as they seem correct as to color and values, they are shaped within the forms that have been previously outlined in ink.*

STEP 3. *Now paint the immediate foreground of the rocks and bushes. This is followed by the foliage and trees of the middle distances and hills. The rolling contours of the latter are roughly indicated, along with the distant mountains. The sky is also roughed in to help establish the values of the mountain, particularly where they meet. As this stage is concluded, the burnt sienna imprimatura still dominates the picture. It is surprising how this stain imparts a substantial feeling to the entire subject. The ink outline is also visible in most of the areas, for the painting is still in a sketchy stage.*

STEP 4. *Make an over-all check of the painting. Once you are satisfied that the color and values are generally correct, begin delineating the various masses. Reshape the trees and shrubbery and paint the rolling hills and distant areas, the brush strokes following their contours. The immediate foreground is painted with vertical strokes to impart the texture of high grass. Paint the sky in a solid manner and arrange the clouds pleasingly. The house is carefully checked with the pencil drawings to make certain that all of the details are right. As the painting is gradually refined, all traces of the original ink outline disappear. The burnt sienna stain still appears in spots, particularly in the rolling hills and in passages where the paint has been applied thinly. However, these are not disturbing notes and justify the preparatory use of the imprimatura in obtaining over-all harmony.*

1

2

3

SALVAGING A PAINTING

Occasionally, a subject painted directly from nature does not come up to expectations. The values may be off, there may be passages of poor color or overpainting in some areas, or any number of causes may contribute to an unsuccessful painting.

Frequently it is possible to salvage the picture by repainting it in the studio while your recollection of the scene is still fresh. In spite of occasional unhappy results, you can gain consolation in the fact that you observed nature, you made a composition, and you obtained a general color effect. All of these factors will prove of value when you repaint the scene in your studio.

The first thing to do is to scrape the entire canvas with your palette knife before the paint has dried or become tacky. Enough pressure should be applied with the knife to remove the surplus paint, yet leave a blurred image of the over-all color effect. If care is taken when removing the paint, the canvas will still retain the general distribution of the light and dark areas as well as an indication of the color.

On the left are illustrated the first three steps taken in the studio to salvage a subject that has been painted directly from nature.

1. All of the surplus paint is scraped off the canvas while it is still wet. Although this step can be taken while still on the spot, it is better to wait until returning to the studio. Then, with a fresh eye, the subject can be reconsidered, its failure to come up to expectations reviewed, and a last mental note fixed before the scraping process starts.

2. Upon the removal of the surplus paint you can proceed immediately with the repainting or wait for the scraped canvas to dry. The disadvantage of the latter method is that the time needed for the drying period dims the fresh impression of the scene as it appeared in nature. If your intention is just to produce a studio painting, this interval does not matter. However, if a replica of the subject as you interpreted it from nature is desired, then proceed at once to this second step.

The reorganization of the canvas is started with the repainting of the principal objects.

What we are doing is re-establishing the significant shapes that make up the composition of the picture.

The immediate foreground shapes are redrawn, including the painting of the two boats and the boathouse. The scaffolding of the wharf is indicated.

3. We continue with the repainting of the distance and the water. It will be noted that up to this point the entire key is low; we are not painting to the white of the original canvas but over a varied toned surface that has been produced by the previous scraping. The light falling upon the flat areas of the foreground, boats, docks, and middleground is now painted.

4. Gradually the entire canvas is repainted, retaining any areas from the original painting that are in correct value and color. At the conclusion of this stage all of the large areas are covered except the sky.

4

5. The cloud formation in the sky is now redesigned and painted. The over-all effect is gradually refined and details added as they are needed until the canvas attains the desired finish.

I should add here that it is not always disadvantageous to have a lapse of time between the scraping of the canvas and its later repainting. The time lag forces you to bring your imagination into play, and this stimulation frequently results in an entirely different interpretation of the subject.

This interpretation in turn can be one that is far superior to a merely satisfying painting of the subject on the spot.

THE AMATEUR PAINTER

Much publicity has been given to the increasing prevalence of the amateur in art. Whether described as a Sunday painter, part-time dabbler, or weekend painter, there is no doubt that he has found a place in the art world. The professional art magazines run regular monthly columns devoted to the amateur painter, and frequently articles singling out national figures who dabble in art are featured in newspapers and magazines. Regional and national contests are sponsored for those who paint as a hobby.

Schools specializing in adult educational evening courses invariably include painting, and the enrollment in such classes is constantly growing. Doctors, lawyers, engineers, professional people from all fields, along with housewives are turning to painting as a means of relaxation. Physicians have organized state-wide exhibitions in which they compete with their fellow-doctors to exhibit in national "finals."

Some professional artists have bemoaned the increase of amateurism in art, claiming that the amateur does not paint solely to please himself but will market his wares at the first opportunity! I do not believe that the financial threat to the professional painter is a very serious one. As many of these professionals depend upon teaching as a source of income, this gathering public interest in art should mean more students for teachers to teach. I am more concerned with important exhibition juries being made up of people who are not professional artists.

The amateur painter can often find interesting subjects in his own back yard. Two such examples are shown above. Views from a window or from an apartment house roof often contain a wealth of pictorial material. Time taken to paint during vacations pays excellent dividends in acquiring picturesque subject matter. Below are shown typical examples of such scenes.

While the amateur may be able to devote only weekends to painting, vacation time affords him an opportunity for more concentrated study. A surprising amount of painting can be accomplished during this time. With fresh subject matter at hand, the amateur painter can produce a daily sketch that becomes a much more exciting record of his vacation than the usual snapshots. Or again he can return daily to continue the painting of a subject, until a completely satisfying picture results.

Both approaches are helpful. Accumulated sketches form valuable material for future indoor painting, and continued return to the subject is most rewarding in learning what takes place in nature.

1. An afternoon is spent in painting the subject on the spot. A rough charcoal drawing precedes the painting to indicate the various objects that make up the scene. The various colors are concentrated on, as are their related values. No attempt is made to "polish" the painting with texture or details; the aim is to secure more knowledge of what is taking place in the big masses.

2. While the above vacation scene can be considered complete in itself as a sketch, it can be carried to greater detail and refinement at a later date. In this particular case I did not return to the spot the following day, but resumed work on it six months later in my studio. As you go through your vacation sketches, you will often find possibilities in them, making it worth while to carry them on to a greater degree of completion. The procedure of using sketches as material for a larger painting is described in the chapter, "Studio Painting."

A rainy weekend does not necessarily mean a loss of painting time. You can set up a still life, which will give you an opportunity to solve many painting problems. Group some objects in a pleasing arrangement: books, a cup and saucer, some fruit and a bowl—anything that is not too complex in shape; place them on a white table cloth and use solid color drapery as a background. Experiment with different arrangements until you find a pleasing composition. Make a careful charcoal drawing on canvas, indicating the light and shade. After spraying it with fixatif or dusting off the surplus charcoal, outline the composition with yellow ochre. You can then make a thin monochromatic lay-in with the same color, or you can start working directly in color, working from dark to light. Place one color alongside another, carefully studying their values before applying the paint, and gradually cover the canvas.

Still-life painting will help the amateur in his color perception, values, drawing, and handling of paint. All of this training will prove most useful when returning to landscape painting.

An approach to still-life painting is shown below.

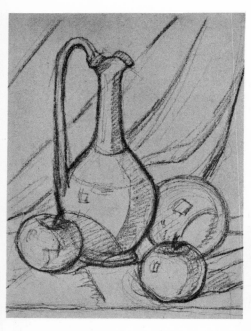

1. Experiment with several arrangements before you decide on the composition you wish to paint. Use simple objects and try different colored drapes for the background. When you find one that is satisfactory, arrange it so that it has pleasing folds. Proceed to make a rough charcoal drawing on canvas, indicating the shaded areas and outlining the highlights.

2. The charcoal drawing is now sprayed with fixatif. Using a single color — in this demonstration I used yellow ochre — cut it with turpentine and redraw the still life, carefully checking the proportions of one object against the other. Then proceed to paint the approximate colors thinly in the shaded areas. This step is concluded with the rough laying-in of the background.

3. At the start of this stage all of the light areas of the still life are still untouched. Then, just as we did in our landscape painting, paint the light areas until the entire canvas is covered. Now check the painting against the still life before you. In all probability some of your dark areas may be off in value — either too light or too dark in relation to the recently painted light areas. Make the necessary changes. The painting is completed by gradually building up the light areas with heavier paint, improving the textural quality, simplifying some of the color passages, and adding details wherever necessary.

VARNISHING AND PRESERVING OF OIL PAINTINGS

Earlier I mentioned the use of retouching varnish to restore the color where it has sunk into the canvas, resulting in dead or dull areas. Such retouching was done in the later stages of the painting to insure an even working surface as well as better adherence of the paint.

After you have completed the painting and it is dry to the touch of your finger tip, cover the entire surface with the retouching varnish. This provides a temporary protection against dirt and also improves the painting's appearance. Use a soft brush as an added precaution against disturbing any slow-drying passages of paint. Be sure that the brush is thoroughly dry before dipping it into the varnish because any dampness may later on produce a milky film in some areas of the painting. The varnish should be applied thinly. Keep in mind that the retouch varnish lasts only temporarily. Another coat can be applied when parts of the canvas become dull again. It is especially advisable to do this if the painting is to be exhibited before permanent varnishing can be accomplished.

Six months to one year later the painting can be given a coat of permanent picture varnish. Make certain that the surface is free from dust or dirt. A varnish containing a damar base is an excellent one both for surface quality and protection.

Place the canvas in a horizontal position. Pour some of the varnish into a saucer and dip the brush lightly into it. Varnish a small section at a time as uniformly as possible, overlapping the previous stroke slightly so as not to miss any part of the canvas. Take care that no ridge appears at the overlapping. At no time apply the varnish heavily; only a thin layer is necessary. If you desire a heavier gloss, the painting can be given a second thinly-brushed coat the following day. Always keep the canvas in a horizontal position while it is drying. Once it becomes tacky, it can be placed face against the wall for thorough drying.

Varnish will unify the entire visual aspect of the canvas by producing an even sheen. More important, it protects your painting from dirt and moisture and limits surface wear. If you object to the gloss of a regular varnish, you can obtain a mat varnish.

Avoid applying varnish on damp or muggy days. Also, do not immediately varnish a painting that has been stored in a cold room. Both the canvas and the varnish should be at a normal working temperature when the coating is applied.

The yellowing of oil paint, which occurs sometimes, often is due to the storing of a freshly painted canvas in a dark room to dry. Exposure to normal daylight will reduce the yellowing. However, it is better to allow a fresh canvas to dry in daylight for several weeks before placing it in a closet, behind curtained racks, or in a room receiving only artificial light.

When you send paintings to an exhibition, take the precaution of tacking or stapling a cardboard on the back of the stretcher frame as a protective shield.

Although most art societies handle submitted exhibits with great care, an occasional careless or unexperienced attendant will place a canvas in a hazardous position. Placing a larger painting against a smaller one can result in the small frame indenting the rear of the large, leaning canvas. The cardboard backing will reduce this hazard and it also helps to keep out dust and moisture.

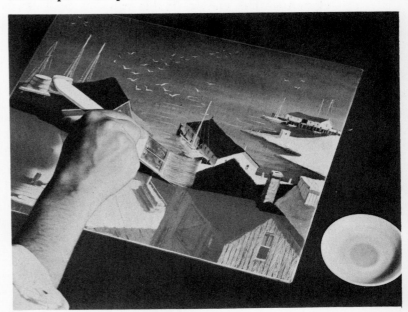

VARNISHING THE PAINTING

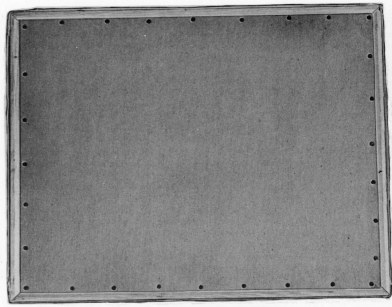

PROTECTING THE BACK OF THE PAINTING

HINTS ON FRAMING

I live conveniently near the metropolitan New York area, so I am fortunately able to view many paintings, ranging from one-man shows to exhibitions of national significance. Each visit is a constant reminder of the importance of framing.

In a one-man show you yourself can place your pictures on the gallery walls, and the effect will be the one *you* want. The subject matter, color schemes, sizes, etc., are all of your own choosing, and in a thoroughly planned arrangement the frames are of secondary importance. They can be a neutral grey tone and simple in pattern, for if they are spaced tastefully, the over-all effect will be favorable.

The situation is somewhat different, however, in a group or national exhibition. Here space is generally at a premium. The paintings often are hung close together and in double rows as well. The frame that looked so well in the studio, or even in a one-man show, becomes unbelievably skimpy on the exhibition walls when placed between two substantially framed paintings. The flanking canvases may be no larger (in some cases they actually may be smaller), but the weight and design of the frames contribute to their impressiveness and minimize the importance of the entry hung between them.

A heavy, hand-carved frame is expensive, but frequently old gold frames found in second-hand shops or friends' attics can be converted to serve for exhibition purposes. Some of the "gingerbread" ornateness can be eliminated or areas filled in with plastic wood to simplify part of the design. Unfortunately, such frames often come in odd sizes, so it may be more practical to locate the frame first and then paint the picture on canvas strips cut to the size of the particular frame.

You can experiment with various finishes in toning the frame to harmonize with the painting. A popular finish can be simulated easily by smearing some indian or light red paint over the gold frame and letting it dry. Then cover the entire area with a neutral grey casein paint, which dries fairly fast. Next, rub over the surface with a piece of medium-grade sandpaper, allowing bits of the gold and red undercoating to break through. The frame can be left with a flat mat finish or given a dull gloss with a paste wax.

From a practical standpoint, however, I would advise you to work in standard sizes so that you can take advantage of stock frames. They are always available, especially in the smaller sizes, in art supply shops and framing houses. The larger sizes generally are not heavy enough, but an inset can be made that will add another inch or so to the thickness of the frame. (Allow for this inset in planning your painting, as it will cut down the canvas size.) If the frame is of raw wood, it can be toned and finished by the dealer, or you may do it yourself if you have accumulated enough experience. The inset—if you make one—can be painted a flat white or covered with linen before you insert it into the frame; thus it will add to the over-all presentation.

There are several good books and pamphlets available on the finishing of frames. The addition of one of these to your library is an excellent investment.

In shipping paintings to various exhibitions throughout the country, the frames undergo a tremendous amount of wear and tear. One way of lessening the strain on the frames where they are joined together is to reinforce the corners. A piece of ¼-inch plywood is cut to the width of the flat back of the frame, as shown at the left, above. Holes are drilled along the edges of the plywood and then screwed flush to each corner of the frame, as illustrated at the right.